TEACHERS
GOV

Kogan Page Books for Teachers series
Series Editor: Tom Marjoram

Fund-raising for Schools   Gerry Gorman
A Guide to Creative Tutoring   Stephen Adams
Making Science Education Relevant   Douglas P Newton
The Place of Physical Education in Schools   Len Almond
Records of Achievement   Geoffrey Hall
Starting to Teach   Anthony D Smith
Teachers, Parents and Governors   W S Fowler
Teaching Able Children   Tom Marjoram
Towards the National Curriculum   W S Fowler
Transition and Continuity in the Educational Process   Patricia Marshall
A Whole School Approach to Pastoral Care   John McGuinness

TEACHERS, PARENTS AND GOVERNORS

THEIR DUTIES AND RIGHTS IN SCHOOLS

W S Fowler

Books for Teachers
Series Editor: Tom Marjoram

For G. F.

© W S Fowler, 1989

All rights reserved. No reproduction, copy or transmission of this publication may be made without written permission.

No paragraph of this publication may be reproduced, copied or transmitted save with written permission or in accordance with the provisions of the Copyright Act 1956 (as amended), or under the terms of any licence permitting limited copying issued by the Copyright Licensing Agency, 7 Ridgmount Street, London WC1E 7AE.

Any person who does any unauthorised act in relation to this publication may be liable to criminal prosecution and civil claims for damages.

First published in 1989 by
Kogan Page Ltd
120 Pentonville Road, London N1 9JN

Typeset by DP Photosetting, Aylesbury, Bucks
Printed and bound in Great Britain by
Biddles Ltd, Guildford

British Library Cataloguing in Publication Data
Fowler, W. S.
 Teachers, parents and governors: their
 duties and rights in schools.
 1. England. Schools. Teaching. Law
 I. Title
 344.204′78

ISBN 1-85091-647-0

Contents

Preface	9
Introduction	11
The Place of the 1944 Education Act (The 'Butler' Act)	11
The educational system	12

Part 1: Teachers

1
Salaries and Conditions of Employment — 17

TASC summary: Teachers' Pay and Conditions Act — 17
Professional duties of teachers, headteachers and deputy headteachers — 21

2
Teachers and the Curriculum — 24

The 1988 Education Reform Act and the National Curriculum — 24
Implications for teachers — 26

3
Teachers and Sex Education in Schools — 29

Sex education and the curriculum 5–16 — 30
Sex education and morals — 31
Sex education and the law — 31
Sex education and the counselling of pupils — 32
Sex education and AIDS — 33

4
Teachers and AIDS-related Problems with Children — 34

The AIDS virus — 34

5
Teachers and Child Abuse   37

Indications of possible abuse   37
Procedures   37
Teachers and school employees involved in child abuse   39
Child abuse and the curriculum   39
Child abuse and action by LEAs   40

6
Children and Drug Abuse   41

Drug misuse in primary schools   41
Drug misuse in secondary schools   41
Principal types of illegal drugs   42
Recognising the signs of drug abuse   43
Alcohol abuse   44
Look After Yourself   45

7
Teachers, Accidents and the Law   46

Professional negligence   46
School rules   48
Playground supervision and school journey parties   49
First aid   49

8
School Inspections and Reports   51

Inspection responsibilities of HM Inspectors   51
Inspections of LEAs   52
HMI comments to the partners in the education service   52
Types of inspections and inspection procedures   53
Inspections of independent schools   54
HM Inspectors and educational standards: their relationships with teachers and their independence   54
Complaints about inspections   55

Part 2: Parents

9
The Duties and Rights of Parents in the Educational System   59

Parental wishes   59

Choice of school	59
Selective schooling	60
Choice of school within the comprehensive system	61
Range of choice of school at secondary level	62
Assisted Places Scheme	64
Nursery schools and classes	65

10
Some Legal and Administrative Issues 66

Children with special needs	66
Exclusion from school ('suspension' and 'expulsion')	68
Bullying	69
Length of school day and school year	70
Journeys to and from school	70
The period of compulsory schooling	70
Absences from school	71
Corporal punishment	71
'Charging' for school activities	71
'CANS'	72
The Law of Education	72
Improving the educational system	72
Choosing a good school	73
Parents as governors	73

11
The Examination System 75

The new General Certificate of Secondary Education	75
Examinations beyond 16 years of age	78
Pupil Records of Achievement	80

Part 3: Governors

12
Responsibilities and Composition of Governing Bodies 85

Outline of responsibilities	85
Composition of governing bodies	87

13
Duties of School Governing Bodies 89

DES instructions and advice on governing body issues	89

*Financial delegation of school budgets
(devolved financial management – DFM)*   91

14
School Budgeting   92

Delegated budgets and the appointment of staff   92
The Coopers and Lybrand Report   92
DES advice on financial delegation   95
*Financial accountability of governing bodies
for delegated budgets*   98

15
Governing Bodies and 'Opting Out' (Grant Maintained) Schools

Part 4: Appendices   103

Appendix I:	Assisted Places Scheme Schools	105
Appendix II	Addresses of Local Education Authorities	112
Appendix III	Annual Governors' Report	123
Appendix IV	Annual Parents' Report	126
Appendix V	Annual Parents' Meeting	129
Appendix VI	Statement of Special Educational Needs	130
Appendix VII	Extract from the 1988 Education Reform Act: The National Curriculum	134
Appendix VIII	Important Addresses	138
Appendix IX	National Parks	140

Glossary   143

Further Reading   155

Preface

Private, public and political interest in education has never been greater than at the present time. Government initiatives culminating in the 1988 Education Reform Act have radically altered a previously long-established 'status quo', a change which has far-reaching consequences for teachers, parents and governors.

The aim of this book is to provide a concise account of the current state of play, with reference sections and pointers for further information and study.

A number of Department of Education and Science documents are presented in an adapted or a summary form.

Quoted and adapted extracts from official material are reproduced with the permission of the Controller of Her Majesty's Stationery Office. The author has used italics to emphasise various sections of the quoted extracts.

Introduction

The place of the 1944 Education Act (the 'Butler Act')

The legal, administrative, professional and academic structures of the educational system in England and Wales rest upon the 1944 and subsequent Education Acts. The 'Butler' Act, as it came to be known, has provided the corner-stone of educational development over the last 50 years and it is only in the late 1980s that further major shifts have begun to emerge.

The 1944 Education Act provided for compulsory free education up to the age of 16, and it laid down that:

> So far as is compatible with the provision of efficient instruction and training and the avoidance of unreasonable public expenditure, *pupils are to be educated in accordance with the wishes of their parents.*

The role of the parents themselves in the educative process was defined as follows:

> It shall be the duty of the parent of every child of compulsory school age to cause him to receive *efficient full-time education suitable to his age, ability and aptitude, either by regular attendance at school or otherwise.*

The role of the local education authority (LEA) was also spelled out in the 1944 Act in these terms:

> *The statutory system of education shall be organised in three progressive stages to be known as primary education, secondary education and further education.*

The principal duty of the LEA was described as the responsibility of providing *sufficient schools* – in number, character and equipment – to give all pupils opportunities for education offering such variety of instruction and training as may be desirable (in view of their different ages, abilities and aptitudes).

As far as governors of schools were concerned, the Act introduced a standard system whereby all schools were to have a body of governors appointed by the LEA.

Strangely enough, the Act had very little to say about the role of the teacher as far as the curriculum of the schools was concerned, and it had nothing at all to say about the standards which could be expected to be achieved in the new national system.

Virtually all the Education Acts subsequent to 1944 may be classed as minor ones in relation to the 1944 Act; it has taken almost 50 years for a new major reforming Education Act to mature.

The educational system

NUMBERS

The educational system of England and Wales caters for a total of approximately seven-and-a-half million pounds within the maintained system. In addition, over half a million children receive their education in 'private' schools which range from small local schools to the long-established 'public' boarding schools.

The total number of schools in the maintained system is approximately 25,500, made up of 21,000 primary and nursery schools and 4,500 secondary schools.

RESPONSIBILITIES

One of the peculiarities of the English educational system lies in the fact that although a department of *central* government – namely the Department of Education and Science – assumes overall control of the service, in practice responsibility for the schools has traditionally been almost completely decentralized.

Thus, although central government has a duty to raise standards and secure a proper return from the investment of national resources, it is the duty of the individual counties and the county boroughs to run the system; to provide and administer the schools; to employ the teaching, advisory and ancillary staff; and to supply equipment and materials for the schools.

To carry out these duties there exists a total of 104 LEAs in England and Wales. These LEAs are required to appoint *education committees* which are committees of the full county or borough council, with additional co-opted members who possess experience in education. As committees of the full council they will have a political complexion which reflects the party political constitution of local government at any particular time. It is thus possible to have a Conservative government but a Labour or Liberal local council, and vice versa.

In addition to the education committee, each LEA maintains a full-time salaried staff which will include a professional director, usually known as the Chief Education Officer (CEO), Assistant Education Officers and in addition staff to deal with such matters as planning, administrative and advisory services.

THE PLACE OF THE CHURCHES

The educational system in England and Wales has developed over a 200-year period during which the Churches and voluntary groups such as the Sunday School movement provided the initial impetus.

Today the Churches' share of educational provision and responsibility remains considerable, since 47 per cent of the schools in England and Wales have church connections or origins. These schools are known as *voluntary* schools: they have been established outside the maintained system but are now substantially maintained by the LEAs.

The main providers of the voluntary schools have been the Church of England, the Roman Catholic Church and the Church of Wales, and these schools fall into the following three categories.

Voluntary aided schools
The largest group is that of voluntary aided schools. In these schools the majority of the governors is constituted from the relevant religious body. These governors are responsible for external repairs and extensions to the premises. The governors of voluntary aided schools have the power to appoint teachers to the school and they also have responsibility for denominational religious instruction. The LEA, for its part, pays the running costs of the school, including internal upkeep and the salaries of the teachers.

Voluntary controlled schools
In this category of schools most of the governors are nominated via the LEA, although one-fifth of the total remains within the discretion of the church body. The teachers (apart from the headteacher and teachers responsible for religious instruction) may be appointed by the LEA, although this right is generally waived to allow the governors to make general appointments to the teaching staff. All the capital costs of voluntary controlled schools as well as the running costs, are met by the LEA.

Special agreement schools

For this relatively small category of schools, special agreements exist between the LEA and the voluntary body. Under the special agreement the LEA pays between half and three-quarters of the cost of building a new school or providing extensions to the existing school.

Most of the governors are appointed by the voluntary body and, although the LEA has the right to control appointments to the teaching staff, there is usually an arrangement which permits teaching appointments to be made by the governing body itself. As with the other categories of voluntary schools, arrangements for religious instruction are the responsibility of the governors of the school.

Part 1

Teachers

Chapter 1

Salaries and Conditions of Employment

Prior to 1987 the position of the teaching force itself was loosely regulated in terms of the Butler Act. Notably, in terms of remuneration the rights of teachers had been encapsulated in the Teachers Remuneration Committee; this was first set up in 1926 under the chairmanship of Lord Burnham and was known as the 'Burnham Committee'. Throughout the 1980s, however, the relative salary levels of the profession continued to fall, while at the same time an increasing focus was being put upon scholastic achievement and standards in the schools themselves. After a long period of bitter confrontation, in 1987 the Secretary of State took the unprecedented step of abolishing the Burnham Committee and the consequent negotiating rights of the profession.

In its place the Government issued a draft order on proposed conditions of employment for teachers, together with an order providing for an imposed and phased salary increase. The conditions of employment order proposed far-reaching changes in teachers' rights and duties, and the orders were only slightly modified in the ensuing Circular (8/87) entitled *School Teachers' Pay and Conditions of Employment*.

TASC summary: Teachers' Pay and Conditions Act

A useful summary appeared later in 1987, issued by the 'Teaching as a Career' Unit (sponsored by the DES under the title of TASC), and the original figures provided a base line for further recommended rises in 1988 and 1989.

SALARIES (AT 1 OCTOBER 1987)
The TASC leaflet outlined the main scale, starting salaries, incentive allowances, additional allowances, headteachers' and deputy head-

teachers' allowances. All qualified teachers other than heads and deputy heads were to be paid on a scale known as the 'main scale' of 11 points, ranging from a minimum of £7,599 to a maximum of £13,299.

Starting salaries

The entry points for newly qualified teachers under the age of 23 were as follows:

- First- or second-class honours graduates – point 4.
- Other graduates – point 2.
- Non-graduates – point 1.

Appointments above the minimum of the scale

LEAs were given discretion to appoint a qualified teacher aged 23 years or over to a higher point on the main scale, taking into account the teacher's qualifications or experience which the authority considered to be of value in the performance of the teacher's duties. However, that point must not be higher than the point reached by the teacher who entered aged 22 years and progressed up the scale by annual increments. For example, a mature graduate who entered the teaching profession aged 30 years could be appointed, at the discretion of the authority, at any point on the scale up to point 10. He or she might also be eligible for an incentive allowance. LEAs could also pay up to two points higher to teachers who take up employment in urban areas.

A teacher taking up a new appointment with a different LEA or who is re-entering teaching after a break in service, could not be placed on a point that is lower than the point on which he or she was last being paid on the main scale.

Incentive allowances and criteria

In addition to the main scale salary a teacher could be paid an incentive allowance on a rate A–E, ranging from £501 to £4,200. The incentive allowance could be paid where the employer is satisfied that a teacher fulfils at least one of the following four criteria:

- Undertakes responsibilities beyond those common to the majority of teachers.
- Has demonstrated outstanding ability as a classroom teacher.
- Is employed to teach subjects in which there is a shortage of teachers.
- Is employed in a post which is difficult to fill.

SALARIES AND CONDITIONS OF EMPLOYMENT

All teachers in special schools (ie schools exclusively for pupils with special educational needs) and all teachers in ordinary schools in charge of special classes of hearing impaired or visually impaired children receive an incentive allowance of at least rate B.

Additional allowances
In addition to the main scale salary and incentive allowances, teachers might also be eligible for one or more of the following allowances:

- *London area*: A teacher serving in the Greater London area or parts of the adjoining home counties was to receive a London area allowance of £1,215, £795 or £309 depending on the location of the school.
- *Social priority schools*: A qualified teacher in a school designated as a social priority school was entitled to receive £201 per annum increasing to £276 per annum after two-and-a-half years.
- *Teachers of blind and deaf children*: A qualified teacher holding a specified qualification for teaching blind or deaf children and who is employed to teach visually impaired or hearing impaired children received an allowance of £501 per annum one year after the maximum of the main scale is reached.

Headteachers' and deputy headteachers' salaries
Headteachers and deputy headteachers were to be paid salaries varying according to the size of the school. Headteachers' salaries ranged from £15,501 in the smallest schools to £30,501 in the largest, and deputy headteachers' salaries ranged from £14,751 to £22,251.

Following the Teachers' Pay and Conditions Act, in July 1987 the DES announced the composition of an Interim Advisory Committee on teachers' pay and conditions of service for the immediate future. In preparation for longer term measures, a Green Paper was circulated early in 1988 with the aim of examining arrangements for a more permanent machinery.

The Interim Advisory Committee reported in April 1988 and recommended improvements in salaries from 1 April 1988; these entailed a general rise averaging 4.25 per cent, and increases of over 6 per cent on some incentive allowances.

The Secretary of State announced on 26 May 1988 that he accepted the Committee's proposals and that they would be implemented with effect from 1 April 1988. The resultant salary scales were as follows:

TEACHERS, PARENTS AND GOVERNORS

Main Scale (at 1 April 1988)

Incremental point	£
1	7,920
2	8,235
3	8,547
4	8,859
5	9,591
6	10,422
7	11,049
8	11,673
9	12,351
10	13,134
10a	13,341
11	13,863

Incentive allowances	£
A	801
B	1,200
C	2,400
D	3,201
E	4,401

Headteachers' Salaries

School group	£
1	16,158
2	16,677
3	17,199
4, 3(S)	17,721
5, 4(S)	18,504
6, 5(S)	19,803
7, 6(S)	20,847
8, 7(S)	22,149
9, 8(S)	23,712
10, 9(S)	25,275
11, 10(S)	27,102
12	28,926
13	30,228
14	31,794

Deputy headteachers' salaries

School group	£
1	15,375
2	15,375
3	15,375
4 3(S)	15,636
5, 4(S)	16,026
6, 5(S)	16,416
7, 6(S)	16,938
8, 7(S)	17,721
9, 8(S)	18,762
10, 9(S)	19,803
11,10(S)	20,586
12	21,630
13	22,413
14	23,193

(For further details see DES Circular 3/88 *School Teachers' Pay and Conditions of Employment*.)

1989/90 FINANCIAL YEAR SALARY STRUCTURE PROPOSALS
On 14 September 1988 the Secretary of State notified the Interim Advisory Committee that Government funding for the 1989/90 financial year would allow an overall salary increase of 5.3 per cent.

Professional duties of teachers, headteachers and deputy headteachers

TEACHERS
The professional duties of teachers were analysed in detail in the Pay and Conditions document as follows:

Teaching
This includes the teacher teaching the pupils assigned to him or her according to their educational needs; the setting and marking of work; and the assessing, recording and reporting on the development, progress and attainment of pupils.

Other activities
Under this heading the teacher is charged with promoting the general

well-being of pupils; providing guidance on educational and social matters; making reports and keeping records; and meeting and consulting with parents.

Further duties were categorised under the headings of commitment to further training; advising and co-operating on teaching methods; maintaining good order and discipline; taking part in staff meetings; participating in arrangements and assessment for public examinations; and contributing to the management and administrative aspects of the school.

HEADTEACHERS

The professional duties of headteachers were similarly summarised as follows:

General functions

The headteacher is regarded as being responsible for the overall management, control and organisation of the school in consultation with the LEA, the governing body, staff and parents.

Professional duties

These were categorised as:

1. Formulating the general aims and objectives of the school.
2. Participating in the selection and appointment of teaching and non-teaching staff.
3. Deploying all staff in a manner consistent with their conditions of employment.
4. Liaising with staff unions and associations.
5. Organising and implementing the curricula of the school (having regard to the National Curriculum).
6. Reviewing the work and organisation of the school.
7. Evaluating the standards of teaching and learning in the school, and monitoring the progress of pupils.
8. Participating in staff appraisal and development.
9. Designing and implementing a policy for the pastoral care of pupils.
10. Ensuring the maintenance of order and discipline.
11. Arranging for information to reach parents.
12. Advising the governing body of the school.
13. Liaising and co-operating with the LEA and its officers.
14. Allocating, controlling and accounting of the financial and material resources of the school as delegated by the LEA.

15. Participating in national arrangements for the appraisal of his or her performance.
16. Participating as appropriate in the teaching of pupils at the school.

DEPUTY HEADTEACHERS
In addition to carrying out the professional duties of the teacher, and the duties assigned to him by the headteacher, the additional responsibilities of deputy headteachers were specified as follows:

1. Assisting the headteacher in managing the school, or part of the school.
2. Undertaking any professional duty of the headteacher which may be delegated to him by the headteacher.
3. Taking responsibility, in the absence of the headteacher, for the professional duties of the headteacher, to the extent required by the headteacher or his employers.

LENGTH OF THE WORKING YEAR, MID-DAY SUPERVISION AND COVER FOR ABSENT COLLEAGUES
The working year is 195 days long. On those days a teacher has to be available to work under the direction of the head for 1,265 hours in total. Also, a teacher must work the additional hours needed to carry out effectively his or her professional duties – including marking pupils' work, writing pupils' reports and preparing lessons. A teacher will be allowed a break of reasonable length at mid-day – there is no requirement to undertake mid-day supervision. Teachers in a school will not normally be required to cover beyond the third day when a colleague is absent.

(This information is based upon: *Schoolteachers' Pay and Conditions Document* DES 1987, HMSO; DES Circular 8/87; *Schoolteachers' Pay, Conditions and Pensions: October 1987* TASC/DES.)

Chapter 2

Teachers and the curriculum

Following the 1944 Education Act, the control of the curriculum rested virtually entirely with the teaching profession as a whole, and the individual headteachers and staff within the individual schools. The sole proviso was that children should be educated according to their age, their aptitude and their ability.

Some hortatory external influences surfaced in the form of reports from the Central Advisory Council, the recommendations of individual subject associations and the publications of the Schools Council. Of more recent interest have been the Warnock Report on Children with Special Needs (1978) and the publications of the Assessment of Performance Unit (APU) of the DES. Nevertheless, the only common external moulding feature of the 1944-84 period lay in the secondary school examination system based upon the syllabuses of the GCE and CSE boards. In other respects, teachers were left as professionals to till the 'secret garden of the curriculum'.

In 1976, James Callaghan – in a rare prime ministerial utterance on education – had hinted at the need for common policies in schooling, and the necessity for some form of 'common core' to the curriculum. Ensuing Conservative Governments attempted to add flesh to this concept, and a plethora of DES and HMI papers culminated in the 1985 White Paper entitled *Better Schools*.

The 1988 Education Reform Act and the National Curriculum

The return of a Conservative Government for a third period of office in 1987 was speedily followed by detailed school curriculum proposals from the new Secretary of State, Kenneth Baker. A Consultation Paper was widely circulated in July 1987 and the concept of a National Curriculum was enshrined in the Education Reform Bill presented to

Parliament on 20 November 1987.

Clauses 1-16 of the Bill laid down a specific and prescribed common national curriculum to be followed by all teachers in maintained schools for pupils from the ages of 5 to 16+ and with the enactment of the Bill following Royal Assent on 29 July 1988, it is planned that the National Curriculum will become operative in 1989. Details of the subjects to be included, suggested time allocations, ages for testing and assessment, and arrangements for detailed working groups to advise on individual subject content, had already been formulated in the Consultation Document as follows.

THE CORE SUBJECTS
The basic core curriculum to be followed by all pupils during compulsory schooling is to be composed of English, mathematics and science.

The majority of time at the primary school level should be given to these three core subjects. At the secondary school level, study of the three core subjects should continue and should occupy approximately 30-40 per cent of school time.

THE FOUNDATION SUBJECTS
In addition to the core subjects, the consultation document proposed that there should be a set of foundation subjects consisting of technology, history, a modern foreign language (not at primary level), geography, art, physical education and music. Taken together, it was estimated that the total prescribed curriculum might occupy between 80 and 90 per cent of the school timetable. The consultation document commented that the place of religious education in schools was already secured by statute and that it must form an essential part of the curriculum. (In an amendment to the Education Bill, in March 1988, it was stated that religious education should be an integral part of the National Curriculum.)

COMPLEMENTING SUBJECTS
Complementing such 'additional subjects' as second foreign language study and home economics, it was suggested that a further number of subjects could be assimilated at 'theme' level (ie health education, information technology), without infringing upon the foundation subjects' time allocation.

ATTAINMENT LEVELS AND FORMS OF ASSESSMENT
In order to provide 'clear objectives for what children over the full

range of ability should be expected to achieve', the consultation document proposed attainment targets for the three core subjects. These attainment targets were to define explicitly what children might be expected to 'know, understand and be able to do' at the ages of 7, 11, 14 and 16 years.

Although much of the assessment should be undertaken by teachers as part of the school curriculum, the consultation document proposed, in addition, nationally prescribed tests which would be externally moderated.

CURRICULUM WORKING GROUPS

Curriculum Working Groups for the core subjects were established in the autumn of 1987, and in letters of guidance the Secretary of State asked for interim reports within three months and final reports by June 1988. *Inter alia*, the Working Party Groups were asked to make recommendations about assessments of performance.

Among his points of guidance, the Secretary of State asked for detailed programmes of study which should describe the 'content, skills and processes which all pupils need to be taught so that they can develop the knowledge and understanding they will need to progress through school and eventually to adult life and employment'.

Furthermore, the Working Party Groups were called upon to state precise attainment targets 'which pupils of different abilities should be able to achieve by the end of the school year in which they reach the key ages'.

The Working Parties were particularly asked to make recommendations as to what might 'appropriately be measured by *externally set tests*. The Consultation Document of July 1987 was 'watered down' in the 1988 Act, in so far as precise time allocations were not specified (see Appendix VII). Professional opinion, however, has led to the view that the implementation of the Act would require approximately the same time allocation formula as that proposed in the Consultation Document, ie at least 70 per cent of the total school timetable.

Implications for Teachers

On the face of it, the 1988 Education Reform Act amounts to a virtual 'melt-down' of the educational system as it has existed throughout the twentieth century. The prospect of national testing at the ages of 7, 11, 14 and 16 years must give rise to serious anxiety about the possible stultification of the curriculum process and its lapse into a process of diseducation, conformity and lack of experimentation. Nevertheless, planned approaches by LEAs, schools and individual teachers can do much to obviate the excesses of sudden centralization:

1. The introduction of tested elements should not lead to the trivialisation of individual study areas.
2. It will be urgently necessary to prepare for the inclusion of testable items as an element in overall planned schemes of work so that the tests will not appear in the form of discontinuous external 'papers'.
3. The testable elements must not be divorced from curriculum obligations in the spheres of attitudes, values and personal and social development.
4. Tested elements should be considered as running across curriculum areas and to varying extents they should reflect a whole staff policy. There is, therefore, now more than ever a need for a 'whole school' curriculum document.
5. Tested elements should not be perceived in a pass/fail sense.
6. The purpose of the tested elements must be made explicit to children, teachers, parents and outside bodies.
7. Diagnoses of learning difficulties, and descriptions of attainments and performance can constitute an acceptable face of testing – benchmarks for the possible failure of pupils (and teachers) cannot.
8. Individual subject schemes of work will need careful and consistent planning at LEA level, at whole school level, at departmental level, and at individual teacher level.
9. It will be necessary to consider 'testing' implications not only in relation to the broad curriculum prospectus presented to parents and governors, but also as part of the more detailed teaching steps which specify limited but progressive objectives.
10. With specific objectives in view, teachers will need to analyse what might be the most appropriate subject content (involving testable elements) and then plan the appropriate learning/teaching sequences.
11. Provision will need to be made for an *evaluation* of teaching programmes at regular intervals.
12. *Feedback*, as far as the tested 'benchmarks' are concerned, will be automatically provided by the benchmark results, but it will be necessary to consider how the results contribute to a meaningful profile of the performance and achievements of the talents and of the competence of the individual pupil.

13. The *interpretation* of the benchmark scores will need the most careful consideration.
14. Teachers will need, more than ever, to maintain accurate perceptions of the capabilities of each pupil stretching beyond the 'levels' of the external tests.
15. For any learning to be fully meaningful it must take place in a setting where there are shared general principles and shared values.

One of the most crucial of the Task Groups' publications was the report on *Assessment and Testing* which appeared in Spring 1988. This report recommended that test results for pupils at age seven years should not be published and that the only form of publication of national assessments which identified an individual school should be as a component of a full report by the school on its work as a whole.

On the question of the implementation of the core and foundation subjects, a major practical difficulty will be the severe and accelerating shortage of qualified teachers, notably in areas such as mathematics, modern languages and science. In this connection the Government has called into question the current concept of qualified teacher status itself.

Chapter 3
Teachers and Sex Education in Schools

Following the 1986 Education Act, the overall responsibility for determining what form of sex education should be provided in a school lies with the governing body.

Thus, section 18(2) of the 1986 Education (No 2) Act requires that the governing body should consider separately:

> the question whether sex education should form part of the secular curriculum for the school

The Act itself allows a governing body to decide that no sex education should be provided at their school; however, the Secretary of State envisaged that:

> governors, as part of their responsibility for deciding policy on the *content* of any sex education to be offered, may determine their school's overall approach to teaching about sexual matters. They should consider whether and how parents should be given opportunities to see teaching materials for themselves and to receive explanations of the way in which they are to be used. They should also have a policy on whether and how to use outside speakers on particular topics, whose contributions would need to be consistent both with the governors' overall policy for sex education and with statutory requirements. But the governors should maintain a distinction between their responsibility for determining general policy on content and organisation, and the exercise of professional skills by the headteacher and staff in delivering the curriculum in accordance with the policy.
>
> As part of their responsibility for determining policy on the *organisation* of sex education provision, the governors may wish to consider the extent to which it should form a discrete element in the curriculum or be spread across different programmes. They will also have the discretion to accept or reject requests from parents for their children to be withdrawn from any sex education to which they object. There is no statutory right for parents to cause their children to be withdrawn from sex education provision.

However, some parents will have strong objections on religious grounds to their children receiving sex education and Governing Bodies should fully appreciate this in exercising their discretion.

In addition to the responsibilities of the *governors*, an increased influence over the sex education policy of the school now lies in the hands of the *parents*, since parent governors will be able to ensure that full weight is given to parental views.

The final responsibility for the delivery of the curriculum rests, of course, with the *teaching staff* of the school, and the DES in its Circular *Sex Education at School* (11/87) rightly commented that:

> The Secretary of State considers that the majority of the teachers involved have hitherto fulfilled their responsibilities in relation to this aspect of the curriculum with skill and sensitivity. The effective discharge of their responsibilities in implementing the governors' policy at classroom level will depend in large measure on their professional skill and expertise, possibly making use of the expertise of health service professionals.

Sex education and the curriculum 5-16

PRIMARY SCHOOLS
Circular 11/87 pointed out that at the primary level care and sensitivity is especially needed in order to match the teaching to the maturity of the pupils. This maturity may not always be fully realised by relying upon the chronological age of the pupils. At the primary level the aim of the programme should be to 'help pupils cope with the physical and emotional challenges of growing up, and give them an elementary understanding of human reproduction'.

SECONDARY SCHOOLS
In most secondary schools, sex education does not appear as a separate subject on the timetable. Usually sex education at this level appears within a wider programme of personal and social education or health education. The Circular pointed out that the physical aspects of sexual behaviour would be within the province of the teaching of biology, but

> opportunities for considering the broader emotional and ethical dimensions of sexual attitudes and mores may arise in other subject areas

SPECIAL SCHOOLS
Questions of sex education in special schools need particularly sensitive

handling. This applies all the more because the majority of parents with disabled children will not themselves have experienced the sexual problems which may be associated with disability. Thus children who have difficulties with learning will need more help in order to understand the physical and emotional sides of adolescence. They will also need to be specially warned about unacceptable behaviour from adults.

Sex education and morals

One of the major problems facing teachers who are concerned with sex education lies in the linking of the basic physical facts to the wider emotional feelings of adults where a relationship between two people involves love and affection.

In the terms of the Circular, the aims of a programme of sex education should be

> ... to present facts in an objective and balanced manner so as to enable pupils to comprehend the range of sexual attitudes and behaviour in present day society; to know what is and is not legal; to consider their own attitudes, and to make informed, reasoned and responsible decisions about the attitudes they will adopt both while they are at school and in adulthood. Teaching about the physical aspects of sexual behaviour should be set within a clear moral framework in which pupils are encouraged to consider the importance of self-restraint, dignity and respect for themselves and others, and helped to recognise the physical, emotional and moral risks of casual and promiscuous sexual behaviour. Schools should foster a recognition that both sexes should behave responsibly in sexual matters. Pupils should be helped to appreciate the benefits of stable married and family life and the responsibilities of parenthood.

Sex education and the law

It is important for teachers to remember, and to ensure that pupils understand, a number of important legal points concerning sexual relationships which are also mentioned in Circular 11/87:

1. It constitutes an offence to make an indecent assault on any person; furthermore 'a boy or girl under sixteen cannot in law give any consent which would prevent an act being an assault for the purpose of this offence'.
2. 'Except in certain very restricted circumstances, it is a criminal offence for a man or boy to have sexual intercourse with a girl under 15, irrespective of whether she consents.'

3. 'Homosexual acts (defined as buggery or gross indecency) between males constitutes a criminal offence unless both parties have attained the age of 21 and the acts are committed with the consent of both in private.'

CONTRACEPTION, ABORTION AND HOMOSEXUAL BEHAVIOUR
DES Circular 11/87 made the points that:

> Schools cannot, in general, avoid tackling controversial sexual matters, such as contraception and abortion, by reason of their sensitivity. Pupils may well ask questions about them and schools should be prepared to offer balanced and factual information and to acknowledge the major ethical issues involved. Where schools are founded on specific religious principles this will have a direct bearing on the manner in which such subjects are presented.
>
> There is no place in any school in any circumstances for teaching which advocates homosexual behaviour, which presents it as the 'norm', or which encourages homosexual experimentation by pupils. Indeed, encouraging or procuring homosexual acts by pupils who are under the age of consent is a criminal offence. It must also be recognised that for many people, including members of various religious faiths, homosexual practice is not morally acceptable, and deep offence may be caused to them if the subject is not handled with sensitivity by teachers if discussed in the classroom.

Additionally, it must be remembered that Section 28 of the 1988 Local Government Act stated that 'a local authority must not intentionally promote homosexuality or publish material with the intention of promoting homosexuality'.

Sex education and the counselling of pupils

It is important for teachers to recognise the difference between sex education in general terms and counselling pupils on individual sex problems. Teachers as part of their duties take an interest in the general welfare and well-being of pupils. In many cases this pastoral care is in addition to, or complements, normal parental care.

Nevertheless, in sexual matters extreme care must be taken to make a distinction between proper pastoral care at school and parental rights at home.

Thus DES Circular 11/87 states:

> On the specific question of the provision of contraceptive advice to girls under 16, the general rule must be that giving an individual pupil advice on such matters without parental knowledge or consent would be an inappropriate exercise of a teacher's professional responsibilities, and

could, depending on the circumstances, amount to a criminal offence.

Wherever possible, a teacher who is approached by a pupil on these or similar aspects of sexual matters should seek to guide the child towards advice from parents. Where the possibility of moral or physical danger or a breach of the law is involved, a teacher would naturally warn the pupil of the risks involved. The next step in such matters may be a question of delicate professional assessment:

> Whether the teacher should take the matter further, by informing the headteacher, and whether the headteacher should consider involving the pupil's parents, the specialist support services, or the local education authority, will depend on the particular circumstances involved and the professional judgement of the staff.

Sex education and AIDS

In view of the far-reaching implications of the likely spread of AIDS, the natural reluctance to raise questions about AIDS at school level has perforce had to give way to providing a general awareness of the problem as part of the curriculum of pupils at the senior stages of their secondary schooling.

Questions about AIDS will also arise with younger pupils and teachers need to be ready with responses to likely questions.

Furthermore, in the view of the government:

> Schools have a clear responsibility to warn pupils of the health risks of casual and promiscuous sexual behaviour – whether heterosexual or homosexual – and of the dangers of drug abuse. Whatever the overall policy on sex education adopted by the governing body, particular attention should be given to the forms of sexual and other behaviour which carry a risk of infection with the AIDS virus and about ways in which risks may be avoided or lessened.

A useful school resource package on the topic of AIDS was launched by the DES in December 1987 under the title *Your Choice for Life*. This package comprises a 30-minute videotape and a user's guide for classroom follow-up. The package is intended for use with the 14-16 age range of pupils.

(Material used in this chapter is adapted from DES Circular 11/87 *Sex Education at School*.)

Chapter 4
Teachers and Aids-Related Problems with Children

The AIDS virus

Because of its extremely serious implications and consequences, it is very important that all teachers should have some understanding of the nature of AIDS and of the virus with which it is associated. The clinical name of the AIDS virus is HTLV-III/LAV which stands for Human-T-Lymphotropic Virus Type III/Lymphadenopathy Associated Virus. It is inevitable that, as time goes on, there will be a number of children in schools who are infected with the virus in one of three conditions:

1. A positive HTLV-III/LAV antibody test.
2. An AIDS-related condition.
3. AIDS itself.

Most individuals who have been infected by the AIDS virus do not have any symptoms and may not develop AIDS itself. However, they do carry the virus and may pass it on to others in certain circumstances. As far as normal school situations are concerned, the DES Leaflet *Children at School and Problems Related to AIDS* (1986) stated that no identified cases of infection were known to have been transmitted at school. Furthermore, the leaflet remarked that research had demonstrated that even in the 'intimate contact in a family setting' where there were children infected with the AIDS virus or who had developed AIDS itself, the infection had not spread to other members of the family. The DES guideline, therefore, proposed that 'infected children should be allowed to attend school freely and be treated in the same way as other pupils'.

Precautions at school

Although children infected with the AIDS virus may attend school freely, sensible precautions should be taken in certain areas: in craft, design and technology and home economics normal hygiene precautions should be observed – similarly, in music. In science, notably biology, antibody-positive children should not give blood for use in class-work etc.

The following guidelines in relation to virus-infected children summarise those given in an annex to the DES pamphlet.

PERSONAL HYGIENE
1. Razors, toothbrushes or other implements which could become contaminated with blood must not be shared.
2. Minor cuts, open or weeping skin lesions and abrasions should be covered with waterproof or other suitable dressings.
3. Sanitary towels must be burnt in an incinerator or the procedure for disposal of infected waste followed; tampons should be flushed down the toilet.

ACCIDENTS INVOLVING EXTERNAL BLEEDING
1. Normal first aid procedures should be followed – these should include the use of disposable gloves where possible.
2. Wash the wound immediately and copiously with soap and water. Apply a suitable dressing and pressure pad if needed.
3. Seek medical advice as soon as possible.
4. Where blood from an HTLV-III/LAV antibody positive child is splashed on to another child:
   - wash splashes of blood on the skin off immediately with soap and water.
   - wash splashes of blood into the eyes or mouth out immediately with copious amounts of water.
5. After accidents resulting in bleeding, contaminated surfaces – eg tables or furniture – should be cleaned liberally with household bleach that has been freshly diluted 1:10 in water. Such solutions must not come into contact with the skin. (NB: Bleach can corrode metal and burn holes in fabrics if used for too long or in the wrong concentration, and must never be used on the skin.)
6. Complete an accident form in the usual manner.

GENERAL HYGIENE
1. Normal cleaning methods should be used; no special disinfectants are necessary for either the bath or toilet. Disposable cloths should be used, and there should be separate ones for the kitchen, bathroom and toilet.

2. Spillages of blood and vomit should be cleared up as quickly as possible. Ordinary household bleach freshly diluted 1:10 in water (preferably hot) should be gently poured over the spill and covered with paper towels.
3. If practical, the diluted bleach should be left for 30 minutes before being wiped up with disposable paper towels.
4. Individual paper towels may be discarded down the toilet. However, if many are used it is preferable to treat them as infected waste. Gloves and aprons should be discarded as infected waste.
5. Clothes and linen that are stained with blood or semen should be washed in a washing machine at 95 degrees centigrade for 10 minutes or boiled before handwashing.
6. Crockery and cutlery can be cleaned by handwashing with hot soapy water or in a dishwasher or dish steriliser.

STAFF PRECAUTIONS

As a general policy, if staff giving physical care to infected children have cuts and abrasions, these should be covered with waterproof or other suitable dressings.

WASTE DISPOSAL

1. Urine and faeces should be eliminated or discarded into the toilet in the normal manner. Potties should be washed and dried with paper towels after use. Disinfectant is not necessary.
2. Soiled waste, ie nappies and pads, should be burnt. If this cannot be done in the school, the rubbish including protective disposable gloves or aprons should be 'double bagged' in yellow plastic bags and effectively secured. Arrangements should be made with the responsible local authority for collection of this waste for incineration.

(The information in this chapter is summarised from *Children at School and Problems Related to AIDS* DES, 1986.)

Chapter 5
Teachers and Child Abuse

Tragic cases of 'baby battering' constantly come to light, and there is now also a more publicised awareness of the very large number of children who are subjected to sexual abuse.

In view of the fact that children spend much of their young lives at school, the problems of 'non-accidental injury' and abuse have a special relevance for the teaching profession.

Indications of possible abuse

Abuse may manifest itself as physical injury, sexual approaches, neglect or emotional disturbance. Signs to watch out for are:

- Changes in behaviour.
- Burns.
- Lacerations.
- Bruises.
- Poor growth rate.
- Deficient nutrition.
- Hunger.

It is important to point out that when a teacher encounters an instance of a problem related to possible sexual abuse, it is usually correct to assume that the child (especially a young child) is not lying.

Procedures

In a consultative draft circular of April 1987, the DES advised that when signs of possible abuse are noticed, teachers should 'with tact and sympathy seek information from the child about the cause'.

Care must be taken in interpreting children's responses to questions as to how injuries occurred. Children who have been abused may have been told by their parents what to say in response to questions and may have been threatened with further injury if they implicate their parents.

Teachers should not regard it as their responsibility to make enquiries of parents or guardians, although opportunities may sometimes arise for raising concerns in the course of conversation. However, if a parent or guardian volunteers information this should be recorded. Opportunities to obtain information are more likely to arise in a school which has positive and regular contact with parents.

FURTHER ACTION

It is important that all suspicion of the abuse of pupils should be reported immediately by the teacher or other persons employed at the school. Such a report would normally be made by the class teacher to the headteacher of the school, or to a designated senior teacher. The report would then be passed to the Social Services Department and it should be received by a named and known member of this department. As a further check, the LEA should be contacted at the same time.

It is also important to ensure that there is a 'second line' of communication, to cover situations where the normal contact is not made, for one reason or another; it is vital that a well-defined chain of responsibility, understood by all concerned, is laid down and followed by everyone.

EDUCATION WELFARE OFFICERS

Where an Education Welfare Officer is the first person to call an alert in an individual case, the headteacher of the school should be informed, in addition to compliance with the Social Services Department procedures for informing senior management. In cases where the school becomes the first link in the chain, the Education Welfare Officer can often provide additional information about the home environment of the child.

SUSPICION OF RISK OF ABUSE

Cases may arise where suspicion of risk of abuse exists. This is likely when it is known that another child in the same home has been abused, and/or when it is known that there is a child abuser in the household. All such suspicions should also be reported in accordance with LEA and Social Services Department procedures.

In a number of child abuse cases which have come to court, difficulties have arisen because of the lack of precise written evidence. It is of great importance, therefore, for teachers to ensure that any observations which they have made are recorded in note form, with additional copies for reference. The date and time of the observations should also be noted, together with an account of any conversations which have been held. If possible, notes of conversations should be in verbatim form and they should be recorded as soon as possible.

INFORMATION VOLUNTEERED BY PUPILS
If a child volunteers information which leads to a suspicion of abuse, the same procedures should be followed. However,

> The handling of such disclosures in such a way as to bring the child to understand the full implications and the need for action, and at the same time to retain the child's trust, calls for great tact and sensitivity on the part of the teacher. It calls for an understanding not only of the child's own developing maturity and ambivalent feelings but also of the teacher's own feelings about child abuse.

Teachers and school employees involved in child abuse

If suspicion arises that a staff member or employee at a school is involved in child abuse, then such suspicions should be reported to the headteacher. It then becomes the duty of the headteacher to assess whether the suspicions may have a real foundation. If it is judged that there is substance in the suspicion, then the LEA and the child's parents must be alerted.

Should an exceptional situation arise where the headteacher is involved in the suspicions, then the matter should be taken to the deputy headteacher who would report the suspicions to the LEA. It is then for the LEA to decide about reporting the allegations to the Social Services Department and the police.

Child abuse and the curriculum

It is for Governing Bodies of schools and headteachers to decide to what extent the school curriculum can make a positive contribution to the prevention of child abuse. A number of strategies, videos and teaching kits have been devised to alert children to measures of self-protection, while positive approaches to such questions as parenthood and social relationships in general can lay down a secure foundation for the future responsibilities of young people. In the words of the DES Consultative Circular:

In the longer term schools can play a part in the prevention of child neglect and abuse through the teaching which they offer. Courses in practical child care skills can contribute towards better parenting. Teaching in the field of personal relationships can help youngsters to develop responsible and realistic attitudes towards marriage and parenthood. The extent to which teaching should be more directly concerned with warning children of the risks of child abuse (including sexual abuse), and with helping them to protect themselves, is however a matter which local education authorities and schools should consider carefully in the light of local circumstances and in consultation with parents and governors. The possible gains in preventing abuse need to be balanced against the difficulty of relating such teaching to the maturity of individual pupils and the risks of causing anxiety and of undermining stable family relationships.

Child abuse and action by LEAs

The imperative need for joint and co-ordinated action in child abuse cases was highlighted again in DES Circular 4/88, issued on 6 July 1988. The Circular was entitled *Working Together for the Protection of Children from Abuse: Procedures within the Education Service.*

This circular asked that all LEAs should:

> draw up in consultation with the local Social Services Department a document setting out specific procedures for dealing with individual cases. This document should be brought to the attention of all staff in schools and other relevant personnel, and new staff should be made aware of it on appointment. Where such a document already exists, it should be reviewed. The procedures should be reviewed from time to time.
>
> Identify a senior officer of the authority as having responsibility for co-ordinating policy and action on child abuse in schools and the Youth Service throughout the LEA, and as the point of contact with the local Social Services Department and other agencies.
>
> Give to the headteacher or another senior member of staff in every school, responsibility for liaising with the authority and with the local Social Services Department and other agencies on individual cases of suspected or identified child abuse, acting as the contact point within the school. The designated member of staff should be responsible for co-ordinating action within the school on child abuse, including liaising with other staff who have designated responsibilities for pastoral care, and where appropriate, for overseeing the planning of any curricular provision.

Chapter 6
Children and Drug Abuse

It is unfortunately the case that the misuse of drugs by children has now reached a point where it must be regarded as a major problem. It is necessary for teachers and parents to appreciate that 'all young people are at risk regardless of age and sex and irrespective of their family background'. (*Drug Misuse and the Young* (1985) DES)

Drug misuse in primary schools

It is rare to find specific teaching about drug misuse at primary school level. Nevertheless, children in the primary school age range are today usually well aware of what is meant by 'drug taking' especially in the form of 'solvent sniffing'. It is, therefore, very important for teachers in primary schools to know enough about the misuse of drugs to be able both to spot the incidence of drug abuse and to be able to answer knowledgeably children's questions on this topic.

Drug misuse in secondary schools

The tackling of questions of drug abuse at secondary level by direct teaching constitutes a possible 'head on' method of airing the problems and offering advice. However, as with sex education, it entails a possible risk of encouraging 'experimentation' on the part of the pupils.

The best approach to the topic of illegal drugs is by its incorporation into wider topics in the secondary school curriculum, such as health education or personal development. The topic could also be raised in the context of physical education. Another approach could be through discussions on the place of drugs in medicine and the use of allowable drugs such as aspirin and paracetamol. The individual and social implications of overdose or dependence upon tranquillizer drugs offers a further 'way in' to the topic of illegal drugs and their abuse.

Teaching approaches to the question of drug abuse need to be varied and designed so that the messages are clearly understood by all pupils in the class. Tape/slide sequences, videotapes, talks by outside speakers and health visitors, and class group discussions can all play a useful part.

In the wider context, the pastoral role of teachers is especially important when matters relating to drug abuse are being considered, as are the relationships between the school and parents.

Principal types of illegal drugs

It is important for teachers to have at least a basic knowledge of the following types of illegal drugs which they may encounter.

– *Amphetamines:* (Known as 'dexies', 'purple hearts', 'speed') This group of drugs acts as a stimulant. They may be taken as tablets or in powder form.

– *Barbiturates:* These are depressant drugs, usually taken by mouth. Their effect is to reduce tension and produce relaxation, but users quickly become dependent upon the drug and the withdrawal symptoms can be very severe.

– *Benzodiazepines:* These drugs fit into the category of 'tranquillizers' such as valium and librium. Usually taken by mouth, the main problems are associated with long-term usage when anxiety and worry may be increased rather than lessened. Withdrawal symptoms include insomnia and sickness.

– *Cannabis:* (Known as 'hash', 'dope', 'weed', 'pot', 'grass') This drug, which is a plant derivative, is usually taken by smoking dried cannabis leaves or plant resin mixed with tobacco. It gives an intoxicating effect and is often used at parties as a 'socialiser'. The use of cannabis can produce relaxed feelings accompanied by heightened physical sensations. The long-term effects include those generally associated with smoking, for example lung cancer.

– *Cocaine:* (Known as 'coke') Cocaine is a powerful stimulant drug which is usually taken by 'sniffing' the white powder form of the drug, produced from the coca plant. It gives a strong but short-lived sense of euphoria and this leads to the repeated use of the drug in order to maintain the feeling. Drug dependence develops rapidly and the effects of withdrawal can be severe, including pronounced depression and anxiety feelings.

– *Heroin:* (Known as 'smack', 'H') Heroin is manufactured from the opium poppy and belongs to the family of painkilling and relaxant drugs which have a number of uses in medicine. To produce its relaxed and detached effect it is taken by inhalation, sniffing, or, for the most intense effect, by injection. The user rapidly becomes dependent upon this drug, and because body tolerance develops quickly, larger doses are constantly needed. Withdrawal symptoms are severe and include vomiting, muscle cramps and fever. The rapid progression from sniffing to injection also carries the added danger of risks from the use of dirty or shared injection needles, and the serious possibility of infection with the AIDS virus.

– *LSD:* (Known as 'acid') LSD is the abbreviation for a synthetic drug known as Lysergic Acid Diethylamide. It is an hallucinatory drug and is usually taken in the form of pills or small tablets. The effect of the drug is to heighten physical sensations and it can produce hallucinatory experiences. One of the chief dangers of the drug is that it reduces concentration while giving a feeling of well-being; it thus renders the user more liable to be involved in danger and accidents. Users under the influence of LSD are referred to as being 'on a trip'.

Recognising the signs of drug abuse

Recognising drug abuse in its early stages is difficult, but very necessary. Almost always, abuse starts as a group activity with schoolchildren, but there are individual as well as group 'symptoms' which teachers should look out for and which will give cause for vigilance.

INDIVIDUAL SIGNS

The factors listed here will, of course, often be associated with 'innocent' matters, but they assume importance when considered along with group and environmental signs:

- Listlessness and reduced appetite.
- Wearing sunglasses at odd times.
- Use of strong scent to cover up drug smells.
- Stealing and/or excessive borrowing of money.

GROUP SIGNS
- Stealing as a group.
- Use of drug 'vocabulary'.
- Regular but brief meetings, often adjacent to the school premises, with someone who is not a member of the group.

ENVIRONMENTAL SIGNS
The discovery of objects, such as the following, will obviously cause suspicion:

- Hypodermic needles.
- Plastic bags (used for glue sniffing and solvent abuse).
- Used matches (flame used for heating drugs, such as cannabis resin).
- Cardboard tubes (for inhaling).
- Parts of rolled cigarettes or cigarette rolling papers (used for making a cannabis cigarette – known as 'joint' or 'spliff').
- Sugar lumps (used for taking LSD).

FIRST AID
Young people experimenting with drugs may suddenly become unconscious and teachers need to be ready to apply first aid, as in any similar emergency.

(The information given in this section is based upon *Drug Misuse and the Young* (1985) DES.)

Alcohol abuse

The topic of alcohol abuse has received a less dramatic presentation than that of illegal drugs. This has occurred partly as a result of Society's willingness to accept alcohol, and certainly 'social drinking', as part of the fabric of life. Full publicity is constantly and rightly given to the catastrophic effects of drink-driving and the increasing incidence of drink–related violence. This can serve as a starting point for an introduction into the school curriculum of the wider problems arising from under-age drinking. Thus in *Health Education in Schools: DES 1986* it was stressed that:

> Work in health and personal and social education courses and in biology should aim to increase the knowledge and understanding of alcohol and its effects on the body. For some ethnic and religious groups in our society the

consumption of alcohol for any purposes is totally prohibited. For those who do view it as socially acceptable it has particular consequences, not least for drivers, riders and pedestrians, which can be studied in various ways; for example older pupils can study the stopping distances of cars moving at different speeds, showing the extra distance travelled when a small amount of alcohol has been consumed by the driver; and subsequent discussions of co-ordination and speed of reaction provide a basis for exploring the links between accidents and the consumption of alcohol.

Look After Yourself

When positive attitudes towards health have been fostered during a young person's life at school, it is worth taking steps to provide a continuing back-up at the school-leaver stage. In this connection the National Look After Yourself Project may be brought to the attention of pupils. The project provides a complete health programme, with the aim of promoting a fuller understanding of health behaviour. Funded by the Health Education Authority, the project has its headquarters at Christ Church College, Canterbury, and the national network comprises over 2,000 tutors and co-ordinators.

Chapter 7
Teachers, Accidents and the Law

During the time a teacher has children in his or her care, he or she is regarded as being in the position of a parent (*in loco parentis*). This position commonly raises a series of questions in teachers' minds as they follow their normal school routine. Certainly, a teacher may feel that there is a practical difference between being an actual parent in a home situation and being *in loco parentis* with 'parental' responsibility for upwards of 35 children as a class teacher, or many hundreds of children as a headteacher.

It should be remembered that accidents will happen and that in the great majority of cases they are simply accidents with no blame attaching to the teacher. LEAs nevertheless insure themselves against possible action by parents or guardians following an accident and all teachers should adopt a similar precaution; this is usually covered automatically by membership of one of the teacher unions. In this context, it is worth bearing in mind the maxim that the man who makes himself his own lawyer has a fool for a client.

When an accident occurs, it is vitally important that the headteacher and the employing authority should be informed in writing as soon as possible; in most cases this is achieved through the use of a standard *accident report* form.

If a parent decides to take legal action following an accident, this normally takes the form of a *civil action*, and it would be brought against the LEA, as constituting the teacher's employer.

Professional negligence

For a case to be proved, it is necessary to show that the accident was the result of *professional negligence*. In the case of the teaching profession, this concept is extremely difficult to prove – all the more so since the 'professional' duties of teachers have proved notoriously difficult to define precisely in the law courts. The touchstone lies in the concept of 'a wise parent' – eg in the case of injury to a child on school premises, could it be shown that the accident would not have occurred if the teacher had acted as a parent could normally be expected to act?

Where accidents are very serious, possibly involving a number of pupils, it is theoretically possible for a case of criminal negligence to be brought by a parent (or group of parents).

Although *in loco parentis* and negligence cases against individual teachers have, as already noted, traditionally been hard to prove and the law relating to such cases has often been described as 'nebulous', as with many professions, acceptance of responsibility requires adequate personal safeguards – especially in the context of contemporary society. This can be illustrated by the outcome of two well-known legal cases which are summarised below.

1. *IN LOCO PARENTIS* AND THE CONCEPT OF PUNISHMENT

On legal questions concerning the punishment of pupils the courts have maintained that a teacher has the power of a parent in respect of 'reasonable chastisement' (excluding corporal punishment).

In a case brought in June 1986 against Lancashire County Council, a parent alleged that his son was being 'falsely imprisoned' by being detained with his class for 10 minutes at the end of school. The parent lost his case, and a subsequent appeal, because the judge ruled that in some cases a whole class could be held responsible for ill discipline and therefore the punishment was not unreasonable.

2. NEGLIGENCE AND PLAYGROUND SUPERVISION

On this question the often-quoted case of Beaumont v Surrey County Council (1968) illustrates how easily an unforseen combination of circumstances can lead to a serious court case.

In this instance, a PE instructor in a large secondary modern school had disposed of a length of strong unwanted elastic by placing it in an open waste bin in a porch near the playground. During break-time on the following day a group of children retrieved the elastic and started to play with it. In the process one end of the elastic hit a boy in the eye causing serious injury.

Damages for negligence were awarded to the boy on the grounds that:

(a) it should have been realised that a potentially dangerous object should not have been left where children could retrieve it;
(b) the playground supervision arrangements were inadequate, with the result that 'fooling around' took place.

It should be noted that the two teachers responsible for playground supervision were engaged in clearing the classrooms of pupils, as the break period had just commenced.

In the judgement it was held that 'it was a headmaster's duty, bearing in mind the known propensities of boys and girls between the ages of 11 and 18, to take all reasonable and proper steps to prevent any of the pupils under his care from suffering injury from inanimate objects and actions of fellow pupils'.

School rules

It is the duty of the headteacher, as part of his or her overall responsibility for the management of the school, to ensure that there is a framework of rules which covers the general care of the children. If a case of negligence is brought against an LEA, a school or an individual teacher, it would first have to be established that this code of rules was deficient.

If the rules were found to be adequate, a case of failure of duty of care could only then proceed if it could be shown that the rules had not been observed on the occasion of the alleged negligence; it is, therefore, extremely important for headteachers to ensure that the school code of conduct and the school rules themselves are fully understood and efficiently acted upon by all members of staff. In connection with the general duty of care of the children, as with fire practice and drill, regular spot checks are necessary.

It should be noted that when a specific duty is delegated to an individual member of staff, he or she is not empowered him or herself to delegate the duty to a further person; if he or she is not, on occasion, able to carry out the delegated duty, then fresh arrangements must be made through the person who originally arranged the individual duties – ie a teacher cannot, without authority, further delegate an already delegated responsibility.

Areas of the school timetable where more than normal injury risk need to be thought of include:

- home economics;
- science;
- craft, design and technology; and
- PE, swimming and games.

In respect of these subjects all schools should have written safety guidelines. These should be clearly displayed and understood by all members of staff, others employed by the school and the pupils themselves. It is especially important that such guidelines should be brought to the notice of newly appointed teachers.

Playground supervision and school journey parties

Additional and very common causes of concern arise in respect of

- playground supervision; and
- school journey parties.

As far as playground supervision is concerned it is essential that a named member of staff should be present in the playground at all playtimes. It is recognised that full supervision for each child is impossible, but the aim is to provide overall supervision, to act as a point of contact and to be aware of possible dangers in the environment.

In the case of school journey parties, the teachers taking part are under the same obligations as they would be at school. Often parents are asked to sign some form of 'indemnity'. Such indemnities are not likely to hold up in a court of law, and the maxim of *in loco parentis* still applies. It is, of course, necessary to ensure that full insurance cover is arranged for all members of the school party.

It is very rare for the case of alleged negligence by a school teacher on a school journey party to succeed, but the Land's End tragedy where schoolchildren were swept off rocks by unexpected waves, and the Salzburg accident of 1988 where pupils glissaded over a precipice, serve as grim reminders that unforseen dangers can and do materialize.

Useful advice on proposed locations of school journey parties can be obtained from the National Parks' Youth and Schools Liaison Officers: their addresses and telephone numbers are given in Appendix IX.

First aid

The importance of effective first aid in cases of accidents is obvious to everyone, but there is, nevertheless, a need for an effective first aid policy for school situations.

Important points for consideration are:

- A *named member of staff* should have the responsibility for regularly checking first aid kits and equipment in the school.

- The *supply* of first aid kits should be monitored for numerical adequacy and contents.
- The school should have an adequate *number of staff trained in first aid* and the total number should allow for such contingencies as staff absences.
- The school premises should include a *first aid room* and all the designated first aid members of staff should have access to it.
- *The 'first aiders' should be well known to staff and pupils*, and their names should be displayed in corridors and on classroom notice boards in a prominent position.
- *The names, addresses and telephone numbers of local doctors* should be well displayed, together with details of the nearest hospital casualty department.
- There should be a routine and easily checkable system for *notifying parents or guardians* in cases of accident.
- *The location of telephones* on school premises should be clearly identified and, in the case of school playing fields, should be known to and capable of being operated by the pupils.

(The above information is based upon *First Aid in Educational Establishments* (1983) HMSO.)

Chapter 8
School Inspections and Reports

The duty of inspecting and reporting upon the education system rests with the DES. This Department of State consists of a small centrally based core of civil servants led politically by the Secretary of State for Education and Science, and composed of a hierarchy of civil servants. The Permanent Secretary at the Department is advised by the deputy secretaries, a legal adviser, and a Senior Chief Inspector of Schools (SCI).

It is only at the Inspectorate level that the DES, in contrast to other government departments, operates on a regional basis and national cover is achieved by means of seven divisions, with a separate group based in Wales. These divisions consist of the North, the North West, the Midlands, the Metropolitan and South Midlands area, Southern England and the South West. Each division has a small network of local offices to provide support for the inspectors based in the division.

The total size of Her Majesty's Inspectorate (HMI) is extremely small in comparison with other similar advisory groups, totalling approximately 485 men and women. Its function, as laid down in the 1944 Act, is to inspect, advise the Secretary of State, and to promote educational thought and practice.

With the advent of the National Curriculum it is expected that the responsibilities of HM Inspectors will be considerably increased.

Inspection responsibilities of HM Inspectors

Under the terms of the 1944 Education Act HMI are empowered to inspect all forms of education. These include all maintained or 'State' schools, all independent schools, and special schools. In the further and higher education sectors HMI have a right to inspect all maintained further education institutions, the polytechnics and teacher training provision.

Other sectors of education which come within the range of HMI' responsibilities include hospital schools, the European and British Forces schools, the education of children in care, education in Borstals and prisons and adult education classes.

As already noted, the total size of HM Inspectorate is extremely small and inspections must therefore be based upon a combination of national priority needs, longitudinal surveys, sampling, and governmental policy enquiries. At the same time HMI aim to keep in touch with the schools which are assigned to them in a general inspector role, and also to be well aware of the structure, aims, and policies of the LEAs.

In the course of a year, a small number of schools and colleges may be selected for a formal or 'full' inspection, on the grounds that HMI, the Secretary of State, or an LEA believe that this is especially necessary and will be very helpful in a particular instance. Additionally, approximately 250 schools per year receive formal inspections as part of plans to highlight particular aspects of education or particular methods of working.

Inspections of LEAs

Each year an examination of the total education provision of three or four LEAs is envisaged as a necessary step towards an appreciation of the overall education system of England and Wales. The choice of LEAs for a report is governed by a variety of factors, with a prime consideration being the usefulness of such reports to the Government of the day, and to the LEA itself.

HMI comments to the partners in the education service

In the course of their work, HMI comment upon what they have seen, indicating good points and how improvements might be made. This is done in a variety of ways:

- by informal discussion with headteachers, heads of departments and individual teachers during inspections;
- by national short courses;
- by publications;
- by conversations with Chief Education Officers and advisers;
- through the published reports which follow a formal inspection.

Types of inspections and inspection procedures

'INFORMAL' VISITS
All visits to educational institutions by HMI are, properly speaking, inspection visits. Some of these visits are made by one HMI, or by a small team: these visits are informal in nature and do not lead to a published report. Instead, a note of the visit is placed in the visits file which is maintained by the HMI to whom the institution has been assigned as the 'general inspector'.

'FULL INSPECTION' VISITS
When it has been decided that a lengthier and more comprehensive account of the work of an institution is desirable, this is achieved by 'programming' a team of inspectors who generally spend a week or so in the school or college. The conclusions of the visit are discussed orally with all those concerned, and also with the governing body of the institution. The written-up report is then sent to the Secretary of State, and copies of the report are despatched by the DES to the school, the governing body and, in the case of maintained schools, to the LEA. Additionally, copies may be obtained by the public on application to the DES (DES Publications Despatch Centre, Honeypot Lane, Stanmore, Middlesex HA7 1AZ). The procedures were outlined in *HM Inspectors Today: Standards in Education* (DES 1983).

> HMI report to the Secretaries of State but first they will have reported informally to those inspected. The reports they write on schools and colleges are now published for all to read, but are specifically sent to the institutions and LEAs concerned. There is therefore no secret reporting and all who need to take action are promptly informed.
>
> When an insepction report on a maintained school or college is published it is accompanied by a letter from the Department of Education and Science or the Welsh Office. This letter asks the LEA to indicate, within three months, what action it proposes to take in response to the report's findings. There may be matters to be put right, but often there will be good practice that requires support and encouragement if it is to spread to other institutions. LEA's institutions and their teachers are free to challenge the findings of inspection reports, or to say what help or support they would require if they are to respond to the findings.
>
> HMI also have their part to play in the action following a formal inspection report. During and after inspection they put their findings to those responsible, such as the heads and teachers, and shortly after that, and before publication, they offer to meet the governors of the institution. HMI also discuss their findings with LEA officers and local advisers, who have a

key role to play in the improvement of education. A strong team of local advisers is often the agency best placed to influence the institutions maintained by an LEA, to foster good ideas, to see the early signs of things going wrong and to give the help needed to put things right.

Inspections of independent schools

Independent schools are subject to the same inspection procedures as maintained schools: newly established independent schools must be registered with the DES and are visited by HMI before their initial registration becomes final. At one time, independent schools could apply for 'recognised efficient' status, following a successful formal inspection. This was not a duty laid upon the Inspectorate in the 1944 Education Act, and the practice has, because of manpower considerations, now been discontinued. Informal and formal inspection visits to independent schools do, however, occur for a variety of reasons, and written HMI reports are, as with maintained schools, sent to the Secretary of State. The DES sends copies of the published report to the school and the governing body or proprietors. Attention is drawn to the main recommendations and conclusions of the report, and a response on action taken is requested. Where necessary, HM Inspectors are able to offer advice and make suggestions for improvement.

HM Inspectors and educational standards: their relationships with teachers and their independence

The principal duties of HM Inspectors are:

1. to report to the Secretary of State on the condition of the country's educational system.
2. to assess the standards of learning and achievement which they observe.

HMI's prime involvement with educational standards, their professional relationships with teachers and their constitutional independence were summarised as follows in *Her Majesty's Inspectors of Schools: Their Purpose and Role* (1988, DES):

> HMI's concern is with standards of learning. The basis for their judgements lies in their extensive experience and they also make use of such measures as external examination entries and results and levels of attainment in literacy and numeracy. They judge whether what is taught is what pupils and students need to know; whether it equips them for jobs and future careers,

and contributes to a better understanding of themselves and the world in which they live.

HMI examine whether the organisation of the school or college encourages pupils, students and teachers to give of their best. They comment upon behaviour, discipline and the opportunities for pupils and students to participate in the full life of the school or college.

HMI do not report on individual teachers. They assess the general quality of teaching and the appropriateness of qualifications and experience of staff. They comment on teaching methods and the suitability of books and material for the needs of pupils and students. But more than that, they look at how well the teaching stimulates interest, curiosity and enthusiasm.

HMI use no blueprints, wave no magic wands. They offer the best professional judgements they can. They have no executive powers. They earn attention by what they are and what they do. Their effectiveness depends on relationships which have to be worked at. Perhaps their most significant characteristics are their professional independence from central and local government and teachers and their obligation to report as they find without fear or favour.

Complaints about inspections

As already noted, teachers may challenge the findings of inspectors' reports. A teacher who wished to do so would normally raise the matter through the headteacher who would then approach the school governors and/or the LEA.

It may happen that difficulties arise during the actual course of the inspection itself. In this case, the best course is to raise the matter immediately with the headteacher who will refer it to the HMI who is leading the inspection team (the 'reporting' inspector). Very often misunderstandings can quickly be resolved informally in this way. It is important to remember too, that inspectors are human, like everyone else.

Part 2

Parents

Chapter 9
The Duties and Rights of Parents in the Educational System

Parental wishes

The 76th Section of the 1944 Education Act stated that children should be educated in accordance with the wishes of their parents. As noted earlier, this parental right is limited by the provisos that parental wishes must accord with the needs of efficient instruction and the avoidance of unreasonable public expenditure. In any event, it is the legal duty of parents to ensure that their children receive a broad and balanced education during the statutory school age (SSA) period of 5 to 16 plus years. In practice this duty is normally fulfilled by sending the child to school. In theory it is possible for a child to be educated without attending school, but this is a difficult and doubtful option, especially at the secondary level where the normal range of studies widens and deepens.

Choice of school

The question of choice of school within the maintained system at both primary and secondary level is one of the most common problems which bring parents and the LEA into conflict. Although the 1988 Education Reform Act is designed to allow a much greater freedom of choice of school for parents, in practical terms choice must be limited by the availability of places in any individual school.

These problems have been exacerbated by increased population mobility and by differing patterns of school provision adopted by LEAs, especially at secondary level. In total, there are approximately 20,000 maintained primary schools in England and Wales, usually with an age range of 5-11 years. There are roughly 1,300 middle schools with age ranges of 8-12, 9-13, and 10-14 years. In the secondary sector there is a national total of about 4,500 schools, usually catering for an age range from 11 to the statutory school leaving age of 16 years and beyond.

In the immediate period following the Second World War, children were selected for different 'types' of secondary schooling (grammar, technical or modern) on the basis of their attainments and potential measured at the age of 11 years by sitting the 11+ examination.

Following the return of a Labour government in 1964, the three-tier or tripartite system of secondary education began to be replaced by comprehensive schools which catered for children of all abilities and usually operated on a neighbourhood 'catchment' arrangement for admission.

Selective schooling

The number of selective schools consequently began to decline rapidly during the 1970s and fell from a total of 1,180 in 1965 to a national current total of 175.

From the figures given it will be observed that there can be relatively few cases at present where a dispute may arise over the non-award of a selective place to a child since so few selective schools now remain. In these isolated cases where a parent feels that an incorrect decision has been made, it is important to gather as much admissable evidence as possible.

Mistakes can and do occur even in the best regulated systems and the parent would be wise therefore to consult:

1. The class teacher.
2. The headteacher.
3. The local authority school adviser.
4. The LEA officer responsible for the area (the Divisional or Chief Education Officer).

Grounds for appeal for a selective place might occur when:

- The child's previous average academic performance indicated that a selective place was likely to be offered.
- The child possessed an outstanding special talent (eg in music).
- It could be proved that the child was ill at the time of a selection test and the test results were strongly at variance with the child's normal performance.
- The family had moved house from an area where a selective place had already been offered.

- There appeared to have been maladministration in the handling of the case by the LEA.
- There were strong and sustainable religious grounds for a selective option in a voluntary school.

Thus, as noted, the first step would be a consultation with the school staff. The next step would be to take the matter to the Divisional or Area Education Officer (in a large county) and/or to the Chief Education Officer of the education authority. A further step can be taken by making a case to the Local Appeals Committee.

APPEALS COMMITTEES
Local Appeals Committees follow a laid-down Code of Practice. Their constitution includes representation from the LEA, from school governors and from people in the area who have educational interests and knowledge. Parents who wish to make an appeal will be informed by the LEA of the procedures to be followed. If the appeal is successful, the result has binding power. However, if the appeal should be unsuccessful, the parent still has the right of further appeal to the Department of Education and Science and as a last resort to the Ombudsman, especially if the case rests upon alleged maladministration at local authority level.

Choice of school within the comprehensive system

Over 90 per cent of all secondary school children now attend comprehensive schools. These schools are of various types and age span and inevitably vary in popularity in an area. Normally children are allocated to the nearest or 'neighbourhood' school and full information about the school must be sent to parents a year before transfer occurs. This information must contain details of the rules upon which allocations of places are made.

At the present time, the number of children of secondary school age is declining and in many cases it is possible for a choice of school now to be given. This choice, however, may itself be limited if a severe fall in numbers on roll compels a local authority to close a school altogether.

If a parent wishes to complain about the allocation of a school or the choice of schools offered for his or her child, possible grounds for an appeal would be:

- A brother or sister has been allocated to a different school.

- The school or schools are at such a distance that, for medical reasons, it would seriously affect the child.
- The parents have a strong preference for a single sex school (this consideration does not possess an overriding weight).
- Another school offers a particular curriculum which the parents strongly desire for their child.

PARENTAL APPEALS AGAINST COMPREHENSIVE SCHOOL PLACEMENTS

The procedure for appeal against a placement follows the same lines as that for a selective school appeal, bearing in mind always that the first points of approach should be the headteachers of the schools concerned, in order to obtain as much preliminary information and advice as possible.

Range of choice of school at secondary level

One of the stated purposes of the 1988 Education Reform Act is to extend further the range of choice of school, especially at secondary level.

In this respect three new factors need to be borne in mind.

1. SCHOOL ADMISSION TARGETS

The Act requires schools to make places available to pupils *up to the total capacity of the school*. Hitherto, LEAs have been able to set admission targets for individual schools at a lower level than their total capacity, often with the aim of 'spreading' out the age groups over a number of schools. Chapter II of the Act describes the new arrangements which will ensure that the admission limits of schools are not set at a level lower than they are capable of accommodating:

> Every school has a standard number, which is either the number of pupils admitted in 1979 or, for schools established since then, the number fixed when they came into being. If the number of pupils admitted in the year before the legislation takes effect is higher, that will become the standard number for the school. The admissions authority (generally the LEA in the case of county and voluntary controlled schools, and the school governors in the case of voluntary aided schools) will be required to set the admissions limit at a level no lower than the school's standard number.

2. 'OPTING OUT' OF LEA CONTROL

Individual schools will now have the right to 'opt out' of LEA control. Schools which choose to opt out will then be run directly, for financial

DUTIES AND RIGHTS OF PARENTS

purposes, through the DES and they will be known as *grant maintained schools*. The procedures for opting out of LEA control were described in *DES News* of the 20 November 1987:

> It will be open to the governing body of any county or voluntary secondary school, or any such primary school with more than 300 pupils, to initiate procedures leading to an application to the Secretary of State for grant-maintained status. A ballot of parents on the question whether such a change of status should be sought must be held within three months of the governing body's resolving to do so, or of their receiving a written request to do so signed by a number of parents equal to at least 20 per cent of the number of registered pupils at the school. Once they have passed such a resolution or received such a request, the governing body must notify the LEA and, in the case of a voluntary school, the trustees. The ballot must be a secret postal ballot. The arrangements will be the responsibility of the governing body, who will be able to seek reimbursement of all or part of the costs of the ballot from the Secretary of State. If the ballot shows that a majority of parents voting are in favour, the governing body must within six months publish proposals for the acquisition of grant-maintained status.*
> The proposals will have to contain specified information about the existing school; about the proposed grant-maintained school, including information about the proposed governing body of the school; and about the way in which objections to the proposals may be made. After a period of two months has elapsed, during which objections may be submitted, the proposals will be considered by the Secretary of State who may reject them, approve them or, after consultation with the governing body of the existing school, approve them with modifications.

(See also DES (September 1988) *School Governors: How to Become a Grant-Maintained School*; DES draft circular (June 1988) *Admission of Pupils to County or Voluntary Schools: Draft Guidance*; and DES draft circular (July 1988) *Grant Maintained Schools: Draft Consultative Document*.)

3. CITY TECHNOLOGY COLLEGES: 'A NEW CHOICE OF SCHOOL'

The 1988 Act gives further emphasis to the Secretary of State's proposal to set up 20 City Technology Schools or 'Colleges' (CTCs). Established in urban areas, these colleges will be run as 'all-through' 11-18 years mixed comprehensive schools. Supported by commerce and industry, the colleges will have their running costs met directly by the DES. The original aim of the colleges was to provide a secondary

---

*This proposal was modified in an amendment to the 1987 Bill, and now provides a dual ballot formula in order to give, when necessary, a decisive result.

education with strong technological elements: by the summer of 1988, six CTC proposals had been announced, and the aims had been widened to include the possibility of arts specialisms. Characteristics of the City Technology Colleges were summarised in a DES document entitled *A New Choice of School* (1986) as follows:

1. They will offer a broad curriculum, with the strong technical and practical element which is an essential preparation for the changing demands of adult and working life in an advanced industrial society.
2. They will seek to develop the qualities of enterprise, self-reliance and responsibility which young people need for adult life and work and for citizenship.
3. They will aim to secure the highest possible standards of achievement, both academically and in other ways.

The effect of these provisions in the 1988 Act should be to widen considerably the choices of school open for parents to consider when their children reach the secondary age. In the words of the Secretary of State:

> Parents will have more choice. They will have a greater variety of schools to choose from. We will create new types of school. Parents will be far better placed to know what their children are being taught and what they are learning.

It will, however, be necessary for parents to keep closely in touch with the developing situation and to ensure that they have all the necessary details from school headteachers, Governing Bodies and the LEA in order that they may make an informed choice for their child.

Assisted Places Scheme

It is important to note that it may be possible for a parent to take advantage of the Assisted Places Scheme which was set up following the 1980 Education Act. The purpose of this scheme was to make provision for children who might not otherwise have the opportunity to be educated at an independent school, by means of an arrangement known as the Assisted Places Scheme. The intention of the scheme is 'to extend choice of opportunity to bright children of less well-off families'.

The Assisted Places Scheme provides sliding scale help with tuition fees and incidental expenses and it would constitute an option worth considering in cases where the parent was strongly in favour of some form of selective schooling.

At the present time there are approximately 27,000 children taking advantage of the scheme, and with an average GCE 'A' level pass rate of 2.6 subjects in 1987, it appears that the scheme is generally benefitting the academically able children who are attending the schools which participate in the plan. The scheme is not principally intended for children with, for example, special talents in music, art or ballet – other arrangements for such children have been in existence for a considerable time. In all cases, the first step would be for parents to approach the headteacher. As places at individual schools are limited, candidates are normally expected to take an entrance test.

For reference, a list of schools currently participating in the Assisted Places Scheme is given in Appendix I.

Nursery schools and classes

There is no obligation for the LEA to provide nursery schools or classes in its area. Many LEAs do, however, provide a limited amount of nursery education, often on a 'half-day' basis. In some cases, where nursery provision is very limited, first choice is given to 'special circumstances' such as home background. In addition to LEA nursery provision, there are many privately run nursery schools and groups at which fees are charged.

Chapter 10
Some Legal and Administrative Issues

Children with special needs

Current provision for children with special needs is largely based upon the 1981 Education Act. This followed a major committee of enquiry whose findings were published under the title of *The Education of Handicapped Children and Young People* (The Warnock Report, 1978). The report stressed the need to get away from the outmoded concept of Special Educational Treatment (SET) for 'static' handicaps, towards a realisation that over a number of years very many children would in fact be in need of some special help. The overall percentage at any given time was put at approximately 20 per cent or one-fifth of the school population. Whenever possible, it was suggested that special needs should be catered for within the range of ordinary schools, rather than by any extension of the existing special schools which, at that time, only catered for a very small percentage of the school population.

ASSESSMENT AND 'STATEMENTING'

The 1981 Act initiated a new system whereby in the case of a child with severe physical disabilities or exceptional learning needs, an 'assessment' procedure has to be carried out by the LEA. As a result of this assessment, the LEA may decide to draw up a statement about what it regards as the special needs of the child. This statement must be shown to the child's parents. At the end of the consultation process the child may be termed a 'statemented' pupil who, as a result of the assessment, should have a place in a special school, or have other individualised arrangements made for his or her education. Detailed instructions on the topic of special needs were given to LEAs by the DES in a Circular in 1983 headed *Assessments and Statements of Special Educational Needs* (Circular 1/83), and the general principles underlying assessment were given as follows:

Although the Act provides that LEAs shall maintain statements only where they are themselves required to determine and keep under review the provision that should be made to meet a child's special educational needs, it places a wider obligation on LEAs to secure that adequate provision is made for all children with special educational needs. The following general principles should apply in all such cases.

The main focus should be on the child himself rather than on his disability. The extent to which a learning difficulty hinders a child's development depends not only on the nature and severity of that difficulty, but also on the personal resources and attributes of the child, and on the help and support he receives at home and at school. A child's special educational needs are thus related to his abilities as well as his disabilities, and to the nature of his interaction with his environment.

The assessment of special educational needs is not an end in itself, but a means of arriving at a better understanding of a child's learning difficulties for the practical purpose of providing a guide to his education and a basis against which to monitor his progress. Whilst assessment should take account of provision, it is important that a clear distinction should be made in future between:

(i) the analysis of the child's learning difficulties;
(ii) the specification of his special needs for different kinds of approaches, facilities or resources;
(iii) the determination of the special educational provision to meet these needs.

Assessment is a continuous process. The procedures followed as part of that process should make it possible to draw on as much advice as each case demands. In most cases, it will be for the school under the guidance of the LEA to decide, in the circumstances of each case, how a child's special educational needs should be assessed and met. Where the interventions made at school do not seem to meet the child's needs, further investigation will be required. If it seems that a child has, or may have, complex or severe learning difficulties which would justify making a statement under section seven of the Act, the procedures set out in section five and in the Regulations must be followed. This action may often arise from school-based assessment, but it may also result from a request by the child's parent, a recommendation by the LEA psychological service, or referral from other sources.

In looking at the child as a whole person, the involvement of the child's parent is essential. Assessment should be seen as a partnership between teachers, other professionals, and parents, in a joint endeavour to discover and understand the nature of the difficulties and needs of individual children. Close relations should be established and maintained with parents and can only be helped by frankness and openness on all sides. The feelings and perceptions of the child concerned should be taken into account, and the concept of partnership should wherever possible be extended to older children and young persons.

Professional advice on a child's special educational needs should include enough information to explain fully the nature of the case and to lead to a proper understanding of the child's needs. The arrangements for assessment under section five, and the form of the statement prescribed by Regulations require the professional advice given to LEAs to be available to the child's parent.

(An illustration of the Statement proforma (Annex 2 to DES Circular 1/83) is given in Appendix VI.

Exclusion from school ('suspension' and 'expulsion')

LEAs now very rarely proceed with the permanent exclusion, ie expulsion, of a pupil from a maintained school. It is the duty of the LEA to provide education for all children within its area. Therefore, if a child is permanently excluded from a particular school, a place must be found for him or her at another school.

It is more common for a pupil to be excluded from school for a definite period of time, ie suspended from the school.

The 1986 Education Act and DES Circular 7/87 provide detailed instructions of the procedures which the headteacher, the governing body and the LEA must follow in cases of exclusion of a pupil:

> Where a pupil is excluded from school for more than five days (in aggregate) in any one term, or if his or her exclusion would result in the loss of an opportunity to take any public examination, the headteacher will have to inform the LEA and the governing body without delay and to comply with any direction given by either for the immediate reinstatement of the pupil. The governing body and the LEA will have to inform each other of any direction given to the headteacher. (*DES News* 7 November 1986)

DUTY OF THE LEA IN CASES OF EXCLUSION: COUNTY AND AIDED SCHOOLS

> When a pupil is excluded from school permanently or indefinitely and the governing body does not intend to direct the headteacher to reinstate him or her, the LEA will have a duty to decide what should happen; inform the governing body and the headteacher of their decision; and when they decide in favour of reinstatement to give such direction as they consider appropriate.
>
> In the case of aided and special agreement schools, only the governing body will have the right permanently to exclude a pupil and they will have to notify the LEA at once.

(*DES News* 7 November 1986)

PARENTS' RIGHT OF APPEAL: COUNTY AND AIDED SCHOOLS

Parents have the right of appeal against a decision to exclude a pupil from school permanently. Such an appeal is made to the local appeals committee. The decision of the committee is binding.

In the case of aided and special agreement schools the appeals procedure could be started immediately the governing body has ratified the exclusion decision of the headteacher.

Bullying

Bullying often starts in a school in a very minor way and although everyone is well aware of the general meaning of the phrase, precise definitions have proved to be difficult – the term may include mental harassment, intimidation, frightening and verbal abuse in addition to physical assault on an individual pupil or group of pupils. Elements of racial harassment have increased in recent times and raise an additional set of problems.

From the parents' point of view, it is essential that any suspicion of bullying should be taken up with the headteacher of the school *immediately*.

From the school's point of view, it is equally imperative that any bullying incidents should be dealt with at once. If bullying appears to be widespread, then it is the duty of any responsible adult to report suspected occurrences to the headteacher and to approach the governors and the LEA.

Bullying often has much to do with the general 'tone' of a school and the efficiency of its academic and pastoral arrangements. A small *ad hoc* sub-committee of the school staff can keep a watchful eye on 'danger signs' and raise questions such as:

- Is the general staff supervision of pupils adequate?
- Could the problem be solved by different timetabling procedures?
- Could the playtime/break arrangements be improved?

In individual cases, a 'case study' meeting may be called by the staff sub-committee. Here not only the sufferers but also the instigators of bullying can be brought together to explore and bring into the open the underlying cause of the bullying.

It must be remembered that, since teachers are *in loco parentis*, they must exercise due and proper care over the children in the school. In the last resort this can entail calling in outside help in the form of the education welfare office, the social services or the police.

Length of school day and school year

The school year must consist of a total of at least 190 days in the academic year, and within this total 10 days of occasional closures are permitted. The school day must have at least three hours 'instruction' for children below eight years of age and at least four hours for children above that age. This time does not include that given to denominational religious instruction.

Journeys to and from school

In order for children to be able to attend school, regulations were framed under the 1944 and 1986 Acts which laid down the distances which children could reasonably be expected to travel to school on foot. This 'walking distance' is regarded as being two miles for children under eight and three miles for children over eight. For journeys in excess of the walking distances, the LEA is obliged to provide transport either by travel passes, school buses or, for small numbers of children, a taxi service.

The period of compulsory schooling

STARTING DATES
Children must start school the term after their fifth birthday, although the LEA may accept 'rising fives', ie children who will be five before the start of the next school year.

LEAVING DATES
Pupils may leave school when they reach the age of 16, but only at the end of the Easter term or at the summer half-term holiday (Whitsuntide). Thus children whose birthdays fall up to 31 January must wait until the Easter closure, and those with birthdays from 1 February to 31 August must stay at school until the Friday of the Whitsuntide holiday. Most children with their sixteenth birthday during the school year will, or course, decide to stay on at school until the end of the summer term after their birthday, especially in view of the final year external examination dates.

Absences from school

Holidays
Parents may ask for leave of absence for their child for the purpose of a family holiday, provided that the total time of absence does not exceed 10 school days (two weeks) during the whole school year.

Illness
Cases of absence through illness should always be reported to the school, but medical proof of illness is not normally required except for absences of over two weeks.

Stage, film and entertainment
Children who miss school to take part in professional performances need to possess a special licence from the LEA. This is known as an entertainment licence. It gives the occasions when absences from school will be permitted and also specifies the arrangements which have to be made for the satisfactory education of the child.

Corporal punishment

Section 47 of the 1986 Education Act provided for the abolition of corporal punishment in all maintained schools, non-maintained special schools and voluntary aided schools. This section of the Act is now in force and all forms of corporal punishment are therefore illegal.

'Charging' for school activities

Following a 1987 DES consultation document on this topic, additional clauses in the 1988 Education Act provided that:

1. Parents can be *invited* to contribute to some school activities – eg class trips or additional equipment – but they cannot be required to do so.
2. Schools will be allowed to charge for the extra cost of activities *outside* the school day. This will not apply, however, if the activity is a necessary part of an external examination syllabus, or in similar situations.
3. *Charging will be permitted for instrumental music tuition* even if this takes place during the usual school hours.
4. *Charging will not be permitted for any other activity within school*

hours, eg for cookery etc. Pupils may bring their own materials on a voluntary basis.

'CHARGING' FOR RESIDENTIAL/FIELD TRIP COURSES
Charges may be made to cover the cost of board and lodgings in these cases. Schools will, however, be permitted to 'remit' the charges in accordance with published LEA policies, and must do so for example when parents are in receipt of 'credit' or 'income support'.

It must be noted that the Act does not *require* the charges to be made: the charges will be *allowable* and it is up to the school or LEA to decide whether to levy the charges.

'CANS'

Particular regulations on school matters are subject to change: For an up-to-the-minute check on individual points, readers are advised to refer to 'CANS' – the *Citizens' Advice Notes Service*.

This reference publication is updated on a regular basis and gives the most recent information on matters concerning the education system.

The Law of Education

For reports on legal cases in education, *in loco parentis*, negligence, LEAs' duties, denominational schools etc, the standard updated work is *The Law of Education* (9th edition), published in 1987 by Butterworth and Co. This reference work can be consulted in most public libraries.

Improving the educational system

In 1985 the DES published a White Paper outlining the Government's plans aimed at a general improvement of the national educational system. Entitled *Better Schools*, the proposals can be summarised under the following eight headings intended to:

1. Secure national agreement about purposes and content of curriculum.
2. Encourage schools to do more to fulfil the vital function of preparing all young people for work.
3. Reform public examinations in the interest of the curriculum and standards.
4. Introduce a new AS level examination to broaden the programme of students on A level courses.

5. Work towards a national system of records of achievement.
6. Make the in-service education of teachers more effective through new financial arrangements.
7. Give school governing bodies a more balanced membership and improve the distribution of functions of governors, LEAs and headteachers.
8. Tackle truancy through improvements in the work and training of education welfare officers.

Following the 1986 and 1988 Education Acts, many of these proposals are now well on the way to implementation.

Choosing a good school

The formal setting out of the duties and rights of teachers and parents has a necessary place in the educational system. Formal structures, however, cannot of themselves ensure good schools. Surveys by H M Inspectors and local authority advisers have indicated that in reality a variety of factors coalesce to produce a reasoned judgement on the merits of individual schools: a significant number of these factors are common in good schools and wise parents and governors will look for the following pointers in their school:

- A good sense of leadership, allied to adequate consultation.
- Full participation on school matters by all members of staff.
- A positive and consistent approach to teaching and learning situations.
- Well-planned and detailed schemes of work.
- Careful monitoring of the children's progress.
- Adequate attention to pastoral care and organisation.
- A relaxed and 'tension-free' discipline allied to a conscious sense of belonging to an institution with a purpose and a spirit.
- Full involvement of parents in school affairs, and an 'open door' policy for help in specific situations.

Parents as governors

Following the Taylor Report of 1977 and the 1986 and 1988 Education Acts, the composition, powers and duties of governing bodies have been considerably increased. In particular, the role of parent governors has been strengthened and parents now make up approximately a third of the total composition of school governing bodies. Conversely, the proportion of LEA governors has been decreased and it now constitutes an equal proportion with parent governors. (Details of the total composition of the 'new' governing bodies are given in Part 3.)

ELECTION OF PARENTS TO GOVERNING BODIES
The election of parents to governing bodies has to be by secret ballot, and parent governors may serve a term of office up to a total of four years. Parents can only qualify for selection as parent governors if their own child is actually attending the school in question.

APPLYING FOR SELECTION AS A PARENT GOVERNOR
In order to set the wheels in motion, prospective candidates should contact either the school parent/teacher association, the school governing body, the LEA or the headteacher.

TRAINING COURSES FOR SCHOOL GOVERNORS
The 1988 Education Act lays upon the LEAs the duty of providing, free of cost, suitable training for all school governors.

DUTIES OF PARENT GOVERNORS
The duties of parent governors are of course identical with those of other school governors, and these have become increasingly wide-ranging following the 1988 Act. In general, governors have an overall responsibility for the school's policy on pupils' learning, the implementation of the National Curriculum (from 1989), the appointment and promotion of teachers, the state of the school premises, the suspension and expulsion of pupils, and the budgetary control of the school's finances.

Many 'lay' governors find committee *procedures* are new to them, and with the imminent increase in the number of school governors nationally, the need for some systematic training on these topics is becoming increasingly evident.

Chapter 11

The Examination System

The new General Certificate of Secondary Education

The year 1986 saw the initiation of an extremely important change in the school examination system at 16 plus.

As early as 1984 Sir Keith Joseph, who was then the Secretary of State at the Department of Education and Science, had called for a new system which would embrace all school children up to the age of 16. The existing external examination system was then based upon the General Certificate of Education (GCE) and the Certificate of Secondary Education (CSE). The differing requirements, and the overlap between the two systems, were among the factors which prompted the Government at that time to press ahead with ideas for a complete overhaul of the system. After a lengthy planning period the new General Certificate of Secondary Education arrangements were launched in 1986 with the first candidates taking their papers in the summer of 1988. Over 60,000 students entered for the new examination, which commenced on 16 May 1988. The first results were published on 25 August and were described by the Secretary of State as 'an important stage in our efforts to raise education standards'. One of the aims of the GCSE is to provide an external examination which covers the full ability range of all pupils at the age of 16 plus and the new examination puts additional emphasis on oral work and the practical aspects of such subjects as science and art and design. Furthermore, class work undertaken during the period of the GCSE course is taken into account in arriving at the final assessment. This course work contributes at least 20 per cent to the final grade assessment.

It should be remembered that although the new examination is a 'single' replacement for the old twin GCE and CSE arrangements, it is only single in the sense of being a single new system with a single set of grades. Since the examination is to be available to the whole school population at the age of 16-plus, a range of classwork and examination questions is offered in order to cater for the differing abilities of individual candidates.

GCSE GRADES

The new examination grades cover a seven-point scale ranging from A to G. Grades A B and C correspond to the 'old' A B and C grades of GCE, and to Grade I of the 'old' CSE. Grades D E F and G correspond approximately to the old GCE grades 2 3 4 and 5.

In the case of candidates who do not reach the lowest (G) grade in a subject, no result of the examination is given and the candidate will be classified as 'ungraded'.

ELIGIBILITY FOR GCSE

Although primarily aimed at the school population, the new examination can be taken by anyone at any age and can be studied for privately or by full-time or part-time college attendance.

EXAMINATION DATES

The GCSE examination is timetabled for the summer period. Some examinations, however, are to be available during the winter, and examination 'resits' will be possible during both the winter and the following summer.

EXAMPLES OF GCSE SYLLABUS REQUIREMENTS

Examples from the GCSE syllabus requirements indicate the types of approach which are fundamental to the new system. (Extracts are taken from *The New Examination: A GCSE Guide for Employers* HMSO, 1987.) The following are examples of the GCSE requirements in various subjects.

GCSE English

The testing of spoken English is compulsory. Candidates may be marked on their performance in a variety of situations, such as school debates, interviews and group discussions, and in the more traditional activities of reading aloud or delivering talks. Emphasis will be given to the inter-related skills of listening and speaking. (Dispensation may be granted for pupils with speech or hearing defects when assessing these skills.) Performance will be graded on a scale 1 down to 5 and will be recorded on GCSE certificates.

Candidates will have opportunities to read, and respond to, novels, stories, poetry or plays, and non-literary material such as newspapers, articles and advertisements. There will be a move in assessment from emphasis on recall of information to a deeper understanding and appreciation of what is read.

A range of writing styles will be tested and candidates will need to show awareness of what is appropriate for different audiences. They will have opportunities to develop their skills in writing letters, reports and instructions, as well as producing imaginative work.

GCSE modern languages

The courses will place particular emphasis on speaking, reading and understanding the language. Pupils will develop insight into, and positive attitudes towards, the culture and civilisation of countries where the language is spoken. They will also develop general learning skills, such as analysis, memorising and drawing inferences.

Courses will test all candidates in speaking, reading, listening to and understanding the language. There will be no obligatory test of written skills for candidates of lower ability.

Stress will be placed on the use of authentic language in real-life situations. For example, depending on the test level, pupils will be assessed on their ability to understand train announcements, to be able to find the way in a foreign town, or to understand the gist of a newspaper article. Individual syllabuses will define closely the tasks, topics, vocabulary, notions and functions that are to be used.

GCSE computer studies

Candidates are encouraged to make use of pre-written software and software packages – including spreadsheets and word processors – which in the real world would be used to minimise the need for programming. Most students will learn some programming but it will be firmly based on good practice arising from problem-solving.

Candidates will be expected to study a range of computer applications through simulations and through observing actual industrial and commercial systems. This study, linked with essentially practical problem-solving, will give students a firm base for further study or for putting their knowledge to work in dealing with problems arising in other subjects.

GCSE geography

All syllabuses will contain:

(a) first hand study of a small area, preferably near the pupil's home;
(b) study of contrasting areas/themes within the British Isles, including the physical environment, population, agriculture, industry and communications;
(c) consideration of the United Kingdom's relationships with wider groups of nations, such as the EC;

(d) study of the geographical aspects of social and environmental issues;
(e) study of the inter-relationship between people and their environments.

A strong emphasis is placed on appropriate practical skills. Pupils will be encouraged to use a range of source materials, and will be required to depict information in simple map and diagrammatic forms. Techniques for obtaining, recording and analysing data will also play a part in developing a range of skills.

Examinations beyond 16 years of age

Pupils who remain at school beyond the age of 16 usually prepare for the GCE 'Advanced' level examination which qualifies them for university or college entrance, and also acts as a certificate indicating a concentrated study of two or three subjects prior to professional or other examinations.

Additionally, it is now possible for pupils to opt for Advanced Level Supplementary Studies (AS) in combination with A level courses. These new AS courses occupy approximately half the time of the traditional A level course and are taken over a two-year period. They have been introduced with the aim of broadening sixth form studies and widening the career options of pupils. As a rule of thumb, AS courses can count for higher education entry requirements as a 'half qualification'. Thus the combination of two A levels and two AS levels is roughly equivalent to the possession of three A levels. It is of course necessary, in individual cases, to check that any chosen combination is acceptable for entry to a specific higher or further education course.

Quite apart from this AS 'substitution' arrangement, one AS course can be added to an existing A level programme for the purpose of widening future career possibilities again – thus science students may embark upon an AS humanities or modern language course, and conversely, humanities students may well include in their programme of study an AS course in mathematics or science.

The rising popularity of the AS scheme is evidenced by the fact that over 1,300 schools (over half the schools in England which maintain sixth forms) now offer AS level courses. Following the Government's rejection of proposals to broaden full A level courses, this proportion may be expected to increase considerably.

THE EXAMINATION SYSTEM

THE CERTIFICATE OF PRE VOCATIONAL EDUCATION (CPVE)
Courses leading to the CPVE certificate commenced in 1985 and were introduced with the intention of providing a one-year course for those students who remain in full-time education after the age of 16, and who have a vocational bias. These students may have had a limited success in the 16-plus examinations at school. The courses are available both in schools and in further education colleges and are composed of three principal sections:

1. The Core;
2. Vocational Studies;
3. Additional Studies.

The Core relates to the basic skills necessary for working adult life and is developed through vocational studies. Vocational studies include work experience and here students develop their interests in business services, technical services, production, customer services and distribution.

Additional studies can include recreational pursuits or additional examination work, possibly for a single GCSE subject. At the end of the year students receive a *certificate of achievement*, which details their success on the course. There is no pass/fail examination system attached to the course.

COLLEGE EXAMINATIONS
Vocational courses leading to examination qualifications usually come within the province of the further education system and awards are secured by attendance at local or regional further education colleges or polytechnics.

The principal vocational courses come within the arrangements of the *Business and Technician Education Council (BTEC)*. BTEC covers such subjects as business, construction, art and design, hotel and catering, and engineering etc. The courses operate in the following three stages:

- *BTEC (First)* – this level can be undertaken without any previous entry requirements.
- *BTEC (National)* – the entry requirements here consist either of a BTEC First, or a GCSE qualification.
- *BTEC (Higher)* – the entry requirement at this level is the possession of a BTEC National or A level qualification.

Apart from BTEC, a very full range of vocational courses operates through the City and Guilds of London Institute (CGLI). Areas covered by CGLI include such topics as hairdressing, textiles, printing, radio and TV, motor vehicle maintenance etc. In all, over 200 course topics are catered for in City and Guilds courses.

ROYAL SOCIETY OF ARTS
A further range of widely used courses lead to awards from the Royal Society of Arts (RSA), with the most popular being in office skills, typewriting and support services for the world of business and commerce.

QUALIFYING EXAMINATIONS
Qualifying examinations for professions such as nursing, law, teaching, accountancy and medicine have their own specific entry and course requirements. For further information, the simplest procedure is to begin by consulting the local public library advice desk.

The Department of Education and Science issues a number of useful pamphlets on such topics as *The New Examination, A GCSE Guide for Employers*, and a careers pamphlet under the title of *It's Your Choice*.

CAREERS
The Careers Research and Advisory Centre (CRAC) publishes much informative material. It can be consulted in public libraries and is a very useful addition to whatever may be offered by way of careers advice through the LEA Careers Service to schools.

(Useful further reading in this area is contained in Felicity Taylor (1987) *After School* published by Kogan Page.)

Pupil Records of Achievement

In 1984 the Government issued a policy statement on the topic of Records of Achievement with the objective of establishing arrangements by which all children at secondary level would obtain a record of their achievement. The operative date was set at 1990, and an interim progress report from the National Steering Committee was published in November 1987.

The proposed records are intended to operate alongside the evidence which will be available from the national curriculum assessments. Achievement records, in the words of the Government, 'will have an important role in recording performance and profiling a pupil's

THE EXAMINATION SYSTEM

achievements across and beyond the national curriculum'. The policy statement indicated that pupils' records of achievement should contain:

1. information (apart from academic success) relating to the personal experiences and achievements of the pupil;
2. a record of the pupil's academic achievements in the subjects of the curriculum and in his or her general learning.

It should be noted that the Records of Achievement are intended to be structured in such a way that aspects of confidentiality and privacy are protected. With this proviso in mind, it is likely that the new Records of Achievement will, nevertheless, make a valuable contribution to the 'portmanteau' of information which pupils will possess, and be able to use profitably, when they leave school.

(Useful further reading is the DES document *Records of Achievement: An Interim Report* HMSO, November 1987.)

Part 3

Governors

Chapter 12

Responsibilities and Composition of Governing Bodies

All county and voluntary schools are required by law to have a governing body.

Prior to the setting up of the governing body of a school, two legal processes have to be completed. First, it is necessary for the LEA to draw up what is known as an *instrument of government*. The instrument of government sets out the composition of the governing body and details the arrangements for the meetings of the governors.

The second step in the setting up of a governing body relates to what are known as the *articles of government*. The articles of government detail the duties of the governing body and the distribution of responsibilities between the LEA, the governing body itself and the headteacher of the school.

In the case of *voluntary schools* these instruments and articles are drawn up by the 'foundation' rather than the LEA itself.

Outline of responsibilities

Following the implementation of the 1986 and 1988 Education Acts, up to 300,000 school governors are now needed. The following 'thumbnail' summary of their responsibilities was given in the DES leaflet *School Governors: A New Role* (DES, 1988)

Governors:

1. are responsible for the general conduct of the school,
2. must have a view on the appropriate curriculum for the school, in the light of the local authority's general policies,
3. decide whether sex education should be provided at the school,
4. may offer the headteacher general principles to follow in determining a policy on discipline,
5. have control over a sum of money handed down to them by the local

authority, to cover expenditure on books, equipment and stationery,
6. may take part in the procedures for selecting the school's staff,
7. must make information about the school available to parents,
8. are responsible for preparing an annual report to parents and for holding an annual meeting with the parents to discuss the report and any other matters concerning the running of the school.

At voluntary aided schools, governors have responsibility in addition for:

9. controlling the content of the curriculum, and determining the nature of religious instruction,
10. deciding which children should be admitted to the school,
11. employing staff,
12. keeping the building in good repair.

Agenda for the termly governors' meeting

In practice the termly meeting of school governing bodies is likely to be concerned with a range of detail. Thus a typical agenda paper might be:

1. Apologies for absence.
2. Agreement to and signing of the minutes of the previous meeting.
3. Discussion of items remaining 'active' or needing follow-up from the minutes.
4. Consideration of correspondence and other communications made to the chairman: report of chairman's actions taken.
5. LEA business: discussion on possible expansion/contraction of the size of the school.
6. Headteacher's business: plans for the coming year; staff shortages in areas of the curriculum.
7. Parent governors' business: state of school playground.
8. Business raised by individual governors: range of newspapers available in the school library. Matters brought to the attention of governors by school parents.
9. Other business (AOB).
10. Date and time of next meeting.

Governors' knowledge of the school

To be an effective governor it is necessary both to gain some up-to-date awareness of contemporary educational concepts and problems, and even more importantly, to get to know the workings of the school itself. Some time must be spent visiting the school and following up special areas of interest – such as the curriculum, finance and pastoral care – by undertaking personal reading.

On the wider issues in education, a governor's personal views may differ from a stated local or national 'policy'. Similarly a governor, as a parent, may find a conflict arises between the interests of his or her child and the general consensus of opinion among the governors – a situation that can lead to considerable heart-searching. This highlights the very real and increasingly important role and status of the school governor.

Composition of governing bodies

In order to increase the influence of parents on governing bodies, and to lessen the powers of the LEAs, the composition of governing bodies for schools of different sizes was specified in the 1986 Act as follows:

Pupil numbers	Parents	LEA	Headteacher	Teacher	Co-opted (or, for controlled schools: foundation/co-opted)	Total
up to 99	2	2	1	1	3 (2/1)	9
100–299	3	3	1	1	4 (3/1)	12
300–599	4	4	1	2	5 (4/1)	16
600 or more	5	5	1	2	6 (4/2)	19

As a result of these requirements no single interest can now have a majority and therefore exercise a predominant interest on a school governing body. Parents and LEA representatives have equal representation, the rights of the headteacher are preserved, and the governing body membership is more broadly based through the co-option procedures and the representation of local business and commercial interests.

The importance which the government attached to the new membership of governing bodies was expressed as follows:

> Under the Act, the governing body of each of the 30,000 maintained primary and secondary schools in England and Wales will be re-established as the main focus for its school's life and sense of purpose.
> Parents will have a greater say in the running of their children's schools.

TEACHERS, PARENTS AND GOVERNORS

They will have a stronger voice on governing bodies which will no longer be dominated by local education authority representatives. All parents will receive an annual report from the governing body and have the chance to discuss this at an annual meeting.

The responsibilities of school governing bodies and headteachers in the running of schools will be clarified and strengthened.

COMPOSITION OF GOVERNING BODIES OF VOLUNTARY AND SPECIAL AGREEMENT SCHOOLS

It should be noted that the new membership proposals for governing bodies apply only to county schools: in the case of voluntary aided and special agreement schools the composition of the school governing body is not altered by the 1986 Act.

TRAINING FOR MEMBERS OF GOVERNING BODIES

Under Section 57 of the 1986 Act, LEAs are obliged to provide, free of charge, *appropriate information and training for school governors.*

Chapter 13
Duties of School Governing Bodies

DES instructions and advice on governing body issues

Detailed advice was given in sections of the 1986 and 1988 Education Acts and also in DES Circular 8/86.

CONDUCT OF THE SCHOOL
The governing body has the duty of controlling the conduct of the school in general terms (this is subject to statutory provisions).

CURRICULUM POLICY
Governors are required to define and keep up to date the secular curriculum for their school in the light of the LEA's policy and in consultation with the headteacher. Following the 1988 Education Act (Clause 6), school governors

> must exercise their functions to secure that the national curriculum is implemented in all maintained schools; that only approved qualifications are offered to pupils... Until such date as the national curriculum has been established for any core or foundation subject, it is to be taught for a reasonable time in every maintained school.

It should be noted it will not be possible for governors to modify the national curriculum.

SEX EDUCATION
> The governing body will have to consider separately, while having regard to the LEA's statement under Section 17 of this Act (1986 Act) whether sex education should form part of the curriculum of the school. They will have a duty to maintain a written statement of how sex education should be taught, and to set down any decision they may make for it not to form part of the curriculum. Again, the statement will be available for inspection at the school.

Conduct of Pupils

A written statement of general principles governing the conduct of pupils should be provided for the headteacher by the governing body. The statement of general principles should include measures to be taken with a view to:

(a) promoting, among pupils, self-discipline and proper regard for authority
(b) encouraging good behaviour on the part of pupils
(c) securing that the standard of behaviour of pupils is acceptable
(d) regulating the conduct of pupils.

Exclusions from School

Questions of school exclusion were dealt with in Sections 23-25 of the 1986 Act as follows:

> Where a pupil is excluded from school for more than five days (in aggregate) in any one term, or if his or her exclusion would result in the loss of an opportunity to take any public examination, the headteacher will have to inform the LEA and the governing body without delay and to comply with any direction given by either for the immediate reinstatement of the pupil. The governing body and the LEA will have to inform each other of any direction given to the headteacher.
>
> When a pupil is excluded from school permanently or indefinitely and the governing body do not intend to direct the headteacher to reinstate him or her, the LEA will have a duty to decide what should happen; inform the governing body and the headteacher of their decision; and when they decide in favour of reinstatement to give such direction as they consider appropriate. In the case of aided and special agreement schools, only the governing body will have the right permanently to exclude a pupil and they will have to notify the LEA at once.

Right of Appeal by Parents Against Permanent Exclusion

Section 26 of the 1986 Act provided a right of appeal for the parents of a pupil who has been permanently excluded from a school, and also for the governing body if the LEA orders his or her reinstatement. Appeals should be made to the local appeals committtee and the decision reached is binding on the persons concerned.

Appointment of Staff

The governing body of a school is responsible for the selection and interviewing of candidates and the recommendation of appointments to the local education authority.

Annual report of governing body to parents and annual parents' meeting

Governing bodies are required to prepare an annual report to parents and also to hold an annual meeting of parents in order to discuss the report. It should be noted that, at this meeting, parents may pass resolutions on matters which require the attention of the governing body, LEA or headteacher.

Further guidance on the topics of the governors' annual report and parents' meeting was given in DES Circular 8/86 of 19 December 1986 and the relevant sections of this circular are reproduced for reference in Appendix V.

Reports by governing bodies to the local education authority

Under the 1986 Act, LEAs are entitled to require reports from school governing bodies, and in turn the school governing body may require a report from the headteacher of the school.

Reports by the governing body to the Secretary of State

Section 56 of the 1986 Act provided that the governing bodies of county and voluntary schools should be responsible for reports, returns and information to the Secretary of State, as he may require.

Governing bodies and the running costs of schools

The LEA is required to make an annual statement of the running costs of the school to the governing body. The LEA must also make available to the governing body, monies for expenditure on such items as stationery, equipment and books. The power of spending the available funds will normally be delegated by the governing body to the headteacher.

Financial delegation of school budgets (devolved financial management – DFM)

The 1988 Act provides for the delegation to school governing bodies of the responsibility for major aspects of finance. Thus:

1. LEAs must submit to the DES their scheme for the allocation of expenditure between all the schools which they maintain.
2. LEAs must also outline their arrangements for the delegation of the individual share of the overall budget to each secondary school and each primary school with 200 pupils and above.

Chapter 14
School Budgeting

Delegated budgets and the appoinment of staff

A very important consequence of budgetary delegation will be that governing bodies will be responsible for deciding the size of the teaching and non-teaching staff of a school within the total financial resources allocated to them. Thus *DES News* of 20 November 1987, outlining the proposals of the Education Reform Bill, commented that:

> The governing bodies of schools with delegated budgets will also be responsible for deciding, within the total resources available to them, how many teaching and non-teaching staff should work at the school, and will have greatly increased powers in respect of appointments, suspensions and dismissals ... In county, controlled and special agreement schools, when selecting a new head or deputy, governing bodies will have to set up a formal selection panel and advertise nationally. Governing bodies may delegate their responsibility for selecting other staff to one or more governors and/or the headteacher. In fulfilling their responsibilities in relation to the selection of teaching staff, governing bodies must consider any advice offered to them by the chief education officer and the headteacher, who have the right to attend relevant meetings and to offer advice. When selecting staff other than a head or deputy, governing bodies must include among those they consider teachers whose names have been put forward by the local education authority.

The full implications of the new budgetary proposals are considerable and were well summarised in the Coopers and Lybrand Report.

The Coopers and Lybrand Report

The Coopers and Lybrand Report is a study of the consequences of financial delegation and was commissioned by the DES in 1987. It reported in 1988 and its conclusions can be summarised as follows.

The delegation of financial control to school governing bodies has major implications for the *general running* of schools. The changes are more than purely financial; a general shift in management is needed. To cover this change in emphasis the report coined the phrase 'Local Management of Schools' (LMS).

The underlying principle of LMS is regarded as the delegation of the responsibility for the *management of resources* as far as possible to schools. However, limits of such delegation can arise in several ways: the LEA has continuing responsibility for the education (and support service) provision in its area and other local authority policies may impinge on the education service; there are also practical questions to be considered such as the potential loss of some economies of scale and the sheer mechanics of operating a delegated system.

To arrive at workable conclusions a number of conceptual models were devised to help clarify the issues:

1. *For teaching staff* the LEA role was envisaged as that of a staffing agency for the schools, supplying staff to school and charging them for the supply; the charge can be adjusted to take account of vacancies and supply cover.
2. *For goods and services* of a 'contract' nature, the relationship can be envisaged as a customer/contractor one, with the school (as customer) having the facility to choose the source and level of service it requires.
3. *Advisory Services* can be viewed in customer/contractor terms, but for most of the services the LEA is as much the customer as the school is. Until LMS has matured it was suggested that it would be too difficult to disentangle these roles; the responsibilities should remain with the LEA for the time being.
4. *In respect of premises* the relationship can be seen as that of landlord and tenant, which suggests a split in responsibilities – a split which is not always easy to define.

COMPLICATIONS

These stated generalities were said to disguise a number of 'complications': these include:

- the precise basis for determining the charge for teaching staff;
- the complexities introduced by the expected competition legislation;
- potential changes in the role of the advisers/inspectors with moves toward the latter;
- the community use of school premises;
- the restrictions on capital expenditure. These will need to be relaxed to allow LMS to operate with maximum effectiveness.

Resource allocation formula

The report commented that it was impossible to consider LMS without reference to the nature of the resource allocation formula. It was suggested that in the early stages it would be necesary for LEAs to devise a formula with these elements:

- the primary component where pupil numbers would be weighted by various (and variable) factors to reflect 'need to spend';
- a flat rate, different for each school, which will be mainly linked to the need to spend *vis-à-vis* premises;
- a component to reflect special activities, for example the costs to the school of community use. Furthermore, it was suggested that schools should be encouraged to bid to their LEA, and elsewhere, for funds for particular projects.

LEA framework

The report commented that:

> The LEA will still need to set the framework for school provision in its area and to determine the overall level of resources to be devoted to schools. It will also need to define the formula which allocated those resources between schools; this will not be easy. In addition to providing advice and support to schools, the LEA will also need to monitor its schools' performance and take action if required.

Changes in school management
The implementation of LMS

> will require a recognition that it is school management that is needed, not simply an increase in administration. We have no doubt that schools will need help not only for a considerable transition period, but on an on-going basis. Some of the help will take the form of professional advice and support from the LEA, some will take the form of resources for school-based assistance.

Cost

The report concluded by noting that the introduction of LMS would not necessarily lead to financial savings:

> To implement LMS across the country will not be cheap. It will require both staff time and cash. The largest single component of staff time will be for training individuals for their new roles and responsibilities: local authority members and officers, governors, heads and staff. It is positive attitudes on

which LMS will stand or fall and these can only be achieved with adequate training. As with most training, the main cost will be the opportunity costs of staff time but there will also be the cash costs of any staff cover and of the trainers and training materials. Staff time will also be needed to devise the scheme and the information systems on which it will depend; this will also have cash costs. There is also likely to be pressure for increased costs from the operation of any safety nets in the transition process.

IMMEDIATE STEPS
The report suggested that

> LEAs start their development thinking as soon as possible – without waiting for further guidance. The initial steps are:
>
> 1. to set up an LMS team; to define lists of those functions which will, those which will not, and those which might be delegated
> 2. to start identifying a statement of user requirements for information systems
> 3. to start developing resource allocation formulae so that the effects can be modelled.

Studied in the context of the Report, budget items and their possible delegation are summarised in the table on pages 96–97.

DES advice on financial delegation

The Coopers and Lybrand Report was followed in May 1988 by a consultative document from the DES on the topic of financial delegation to schools. Issued in the form of a draft circular, the document offered advice with the aim of preparing LEAs and governing bodies for the submission of their schemes by September 1989. Financial delegation schemes must be implemented by 1993 at the latest. The framework for delegation was outlined in Section 6-7 of the paper: (DES draft circular (1988) *Guidance on the Government's Proposals for Grant Maintained Schools*)

> 6. The items of expenditure delegated must include the bulk of school expenditure – including staffing, books and equipment and day-to-day premises costs. The Act excludes capital spending and debt charges from delegation, and regulations made by the Secretary of State exclude specific Government grants and a small number of other items. In addition, LEAs may propose to retain central provision for a limited number of other items. The core funding of all schools covered by a scheme, whether or not they have delegated budgets, will be determined on the basis of a 'formula' for

Budget item	Delegation to school	Advice/constraints	Form of charge to school	Other comments
Teaching staff	✓	advice	LEA to charge	adjusted for vacancies & supply cover
Supply cover	✓	—	insurance basis	
Incentive allowances	✓	—	at cost	
Dismissal	✓	—	—	school charged only if 'good reason'
Recruitment	partial	CEO to advise	advert cost + fee	
Training	partial	advice		
Non-teaching staff	✓	—	at cost	LEA may advise on job descriptions
Goods (eg books)	✓	—	direct	LEA may make available central provision
Cleaning	✓	Health & Safety output stds.	direct	
School meals	✓	advice on provision; policy on subsidy	direct	LEA to pay for any subsidy it specifies
Caretaking	✓	Health & Safety output stds.	direct	
Advisers/inspectorate	✗	—	—	possible split later between schools & LEA
Ed. psych. etc	✗	—	—	
Careers service	✗	—	—	possible split later between schools & LEA

SCHOOL BUDGETING

Technical support	×	—	possible split later between schools & LEA
Internal audit	×	—	LEA to inspect
Repairs & maint. (buildings & grounds)	non-structural	Health & Safety output stds.	
Rent & rates	×	—	direct	rates later perhaps if schools have more control
Energy & water	✓	—	direct	
Insurance	×	—		
Lettings	mainly	—	LA to recompense for costs of non-school use	a difficult area
Contingencies	minor eg prices but not pay	—	direct	
Others	mixed	—		see text
Capital	×	—		relaxation needed on constraints

Table 1.
Possible delegation of budget items

allocating between individual schools the resources remaining after deduction of the excluded items (see paragraphs 53-59). The schools' funding will be based on financial years, as is the LEA's.

7. All schemes will need to include four principal elements:
- a clear indication of what is being delegated;
- a description of the basis for allocating resources between individual schools (the 'formula');
- the timetable for the introduction of schemes and phasing in of delegated budgets; and
- details of the conditions and requirements that the LEA proposes to apply to governing bodies, including financial regulations and standing orders relevant to the scheme.

DELEGATED BUDGET RESPONSIBILITIES OF GOVERNING BODIES

The responsibilities of governing bodies with delegated budgets were stated in paragraph 13 of the document:

13. Within the national and local framework established through schemes and the statutory duties of governors, the governing body of a school with financial delegation will control the running of the school within its delegated budget. Subject to these overriding conditions, the governing body will have freedom to deploy resources within its budget according to its own educational needs and priorities. It will determine the number of both teaching and non-teaching staff at the school, will select for appointment and will be able to require dismissal, taking account of the professional advice of the Chief Education Officer, his staff and the headteacher. In aided schools the governing body is the employer of staff and will have full powers over appointment and dismissal. It will be for the governing body, together with the headteacher, to develop and carry out a management plan for their school within the general conditions and requirements of the LEA's scheme.

Financial accountability of governing bodies for delegated budgets

The following is taken from the DES draft circular, paras 84-7:

84. If the governing body of a school with a delegated budget enters into a contract, it does so as an agent of the LEA. This applies equally to the governors of aided schools using their delegated budget within the terms of an LEA's scheme. Governing bodies of all schools will have extensive freedom to spend their delegated budgets as they see fit. Section 28(6) therefore makes it clear that the governors of a school will not incur any personal financial liability in respect of any contract they enter into in good

faith in the exercise or purported exercise of their delegated powers under a scheme.

85. Any contractual liability, for example resulting from the cancellation of a contract for supplies, will fall ultimately to be met by the LEA. LEAs will be expected to include provision in their schemes for charging some or all of such expenses to the school's delegated budget where that would be an appropriate and practical sanction.

86. Different issues arise in relation to the liability of governors for negligence. Section 28(6) does not exempt governors from liability under common law for any negligent action resulting in damage to people or property. One example would be where they failed to ensure the repair of faulty equipment and personal injury resulted. Any liability falling on the governors as a result of their negligence would be joint and several.

87. The governing bodies of some voluntary aided schools currently take out insurance to cover potential liability in respect of their specific responsibilities. Most LEAs do not currently insure against such risks, since they act as their own insurers. In order to avoid committing a significant proportion of the delegated budgets of schools to external insurance premiums, LEAs will have to provide in their schemes that they will act as insurers for school-related injuries or damage.

Chapter 15
Governing Bodies and Schools 'Opting Out' (Grant Maintained)

If a school decides, as a result of a governing body decision, to 'opt-out' of LEA control (see also p 62) and become a 'grant maintained' school, the following points arise:

1. THE GOVERNING BODY
A new governing body must be established with its own instrument and articles of government. Under the 1988 Act, such a governing body must include:

- Five elected parent governors.
- One or two elected teacher governors.
- Enough 'first' or 'foundation' governors to outnumber the other governors. (At least two of the 'first' governors must be parents of children at the school, when they take up office.)
- The headteacher.
- The Secretary of State may appoint up to two further governors if this appears to be necessary.
- The Secretary of State has the power to make appointments to vacancies among first governors on the governing body, if the governing body appears unable to do so.

(*Note*: In the case of former county schools, the new governors are termed 'first governors'. For former voluntary schools the term 'foundation governor' is used. The Secretary of State will not have the power to appoint to vacancies among the 'foundation' governors of a former voluntary school.)

2. ARTICLES OF GOVERNMENT
These must set out the details of the functions of the Secretary of State and also of the governing body. The articles of government must

outline the admissions policy of the school, its duties in relation to the National Curriculum, and the arrangements for appeals and complaints.

3. TRANSFER OF STAFF
When a grant maintained proposal is implemented, staff of the new grant maintained school will transfer without a break from their former service in the previous county or voluntary school.

4. CHARACTER OF GRANT MAINTAINED SCHOOLS
It is important to note that the Act requires that the *character* of the school must not be changed when it acquires grant maintained status. Should any change be contemplated in the future, the governing body must make public statutory proposals. As with maintained schools, objections to such proposals may be submitted.

5. CONTINUING RESPONSIBILITY OF THE LEA
Clause 75 of the 1988 Act requires the LEA to retain the provision of 'certain services and benefits' to the school. Most importantly it states that:

> the authority will be required to treat pupils at the grant maintained school no less favourably than pupils at schools maintained by them.

6. BUDGETING IN GRANT MAINTAINED SCHOOLS
As grant maintained schools will be 'centrally' funded, they will receive from the Secretary of State an annual maintenance grant. In addition, the Secretary of State may pay a grant of 100 per cent for capital expenses and some other types of expenditure. Responsibility for school expenditure overall will rest with the governing body and will follow lines similar to those proposed for delegated budgets in maintained schools.

Part 4

Appendices

Appendix I
Assisted Places Scheme Schools

Alongside the names of each school, arranged by counties, are a number of symbols:

1. The normal age of entry is given in brackets, alongside an indication of the number of assisted places likely to be offered.
2. The number of places at sixth form level is shown with the indication (VI).
3. Boys' schools are indicated by 'B'.
4. Girls' schools are indicated by 'G'.
5. Mixed schools are indicated by 'M'.
6. Schools with mixed sixth forms are shown (M).
7. Schools with boarding places for assisted place pupils are shown as 'b'.

London

City of London School, Victoria Embankment EC4. B. 20(11)+5(VI)
City of London School for Girls, Barbican, EC2. G. 20(11)+5(VI)
Forest School, Snaresbrook, E17. M^b. 21(11)+5(VI)
Highgate School, N6. B^b. 7(11)+5(VI)
South Hampstead High School, NW3. G. 11(11)+5(VI)
University College School, Hampstead, NW3. B. 10(11)+5(VI)
Mill Hill School, NW7. B(M)^b. 14(11,13)+5(VI)
Blackheath High School, Wemyss Rd, SE3. G. 14(11)+5(VI)
St Dunstan's College, Catford, SE6. B. 25(11)+5(VI)
Eltham College, SE9. B(M)^b. 17(11,12,13)+5(VI)
Colfe's School, Lee, SE12. B(M). 32(11,13)+5(VI)
Dulwich College, SE21. B^b 45(11,13)+5(VI)
James Allen's Girls' School, Dulwich, SE22. G. 26(11,13)+5(VI)
Alleyn's School, Dulwich, SE22. M. 30(11,13)+5(VI)
Sydenham High School, Westwood Hill, SE26. G. 18(11)+5(VI)

Westminster School, SW1. B(M). 8(11)
Streatham Hill and Clapham High School, SW2. G. 24(11)+5(VI)
Emanuel School, Battersea Rise, SW11. B. 50(11,13)+5(VI)
St Paul's School, Barnes, SW13. B^b. 15(11,13)+5(VI)
Putney High School, Putney Hill, SW15. G. 30(11)+5(VI)
King's College School, Wimbledon, SW19. B. 16(11,13)+5(VI)
Wimbledon High School, Mansel Rd, SW19. G. 10(11)+5(VI)
Queen's College, Harley St, W1. G. 10(11)+5(VI)
St Benedict's RC School, Ealing, W5. B(M). 10(11)+5(VI)
Godolphin and Latymer School, Hammersmith, W6. G. 35(11)+5(VI)
Latymer Upper School, Hammersmith, W6. B. 50(11)+5(VI)
St Paul's Girls School, Hammersmith, W6. G. 10(11)+5(VI)
Notting Hill and Ealing High School, W13. G. 18(11)+5(VI)

Surrey, Kent and Sussex

King Edward's School, Witley, Nr Godalming. M^b. 12(11,12,13)+5(VI)
Charterhouse, Godalming. B(M)^b. 5(VI)
Cranleigh School. B(M)^b. 6(11,13)+5(VI)
St Catherine's School, Bramley. G^b. 10(11,12)+5(VI)
Royal Grammar School, Guildford. B. 20(11)+5(VI)
Sir William Perkins's School, Chertsey. G. 15(11)+5(VI)
St Maur's RC Convent, Weybridge. G^b. 10(11,12)+5(VI)
St George's RC College, Weybridge. B^b. 5(11)
Epsom College. B^b. 5(11,13)+5(VI)
St John's School Leatherhead. B. 5(13)+5(VI)
Kingston Grammar School. M. 25(11,13)+5(VI)
Sutton High School, Cheam Rd, Sutton. G. 12(11)+5(VI)
Croydon High School, South Croydon. G. 19(11)+5(VI)
Old Palace School, Croydon. G. 35(11)+5(VI)
Trinity School of John Whitgift, Croydon. B. 20(11)+5(VI)
Whitgift School, South Croydon. B. 15(11)+5(VI)
Reigate Grammar School. B(M). 15(11)+5(VI)
Caterham School, B(M)^b. 20(11,12,13)+5(VI)
Bromley High School, Bromley, Kent. G. 20(11)+5(VI)
Walthamstow Hall, Sevenoaks, G^b. 13(11)+5(VI)
King's School, Rochester. B(M)^b. 10(11,13)+2(VI)
Tonbridge School. B^b. 5(VI)
Sutton Valence School, Nr Maidstone. B^b. 10(11,13)+5(VI)
Ashford School, East Hill, Ashford, Kent G^b. 6(11)+5(VI)
Kent College, Canterbury. M^b. 12(11,12,13)+5(VI)
Brighton College. B(M)^b. 15(11)+5(VI)
Brighton and Hove High School, Brighton. G. 30(11,12)+5(VI)
St Mary's Hall, Brighton. G^b. 10(11,12,13)+5(VI)

South and South-East

OXON, BERKS, BUCKS AND HANTS
Magdalen College School, Oxford. B^b. 21(11,13)+3(VI)
Oxford High School, Belbroughton Rd. Oxford. G. 20(11)+5(VI)
Abingdon School, Park Rd, Abingdon. B^b. 15(11,13)+5(VI)
Abingdon. B^b. 15(11,13)+5(VI)
School of St Helen and St Katharine, Abingdon. G. 15(11)+5(VI)
Carmel College, Wallingford. M^b. 15(11,12,13)+5(VI)
Wellington College, Crowthorne, Berks. B(M)^b. 8(11,13)+5(VI)
Abbey School, Kendrick Rd, Reading. G. 20(11)+5(VI)
Bradfield College, Reading. B^b. 5(VI)
St Joseph's RC Convent, Upper Redlands Rd, Reading. G. 20(11)+5(VI)
Stowe School, Nr Buckingham. B(M)^b. 3(VI)
Salesian RC College, Farnborough, Hants. B. 20(11)+5(VI)
Farnborough Hill RC School, Farnborough, Hants. G. 40(11,12,13)+5(VI)
Lord Wandsworth College, Long Sutton, Basingstoke. B^b. 12(11,12,13)+3(VI)
Winchester College. B^b. 5(13)
St Swithun's School, Winchester. G^b. 3(VI)
King Edward VI School, Kellett Rd, Southampton. B(M). 35(11,13)+5(VI)
Bedales School, Petersfield. M^b+5(VI)
Churcher's College, Petersfield. B(M)^b. 20(11,12,13)+4(VI)
St John's RC College, Southsea. B^b. 30(11,12,13)
Portsmouth High School, Kent Rd, Southsea, G. 24(11)+5(VI)
Portsmouth Grammar School, High St, Portsmouth. B. 30(11)+5(VI)

MIDDLESEX, HERTS AND ESSEX
Hampton School, Middx. B. 31(11,13)+5(VI)
Lady Eleanor Holles School, Hampton, Middx. G. 15(11)+5(VI)
North London Collegiate School, Edgware. G. 15(11)+2(VI)
John Lyon School, Harrow. B. 16(11,13)+4(VI)
Merchant Taylor's School, Northwood. B^b. 15(11)+5(VI)
St Helen's School, Northwood. G^b. 7(11,12)+3(VI)
Aldenham School, Elstree. B(M)^b. 5(13)+5(VI)
Haberdashers' Aske's Girls' School, Elstree. G. 30(11)+5(VI)
Haberdashers' Aske's School, Borehamwood. B. 35(11)+5(VI)
St Albans School, Abbey Gateway, St Albans, B. 20(11)+5(VI)
St Albans High School, Townsend Ave, St Albans. G. 10(11)+5(VI)
Berkhamsted School. B^b. 6(11,13)+2(VI)
Berkhamsted School for Girls. G. 6(11)+5(VI)
St Edmund's RC College, Ware. B(M)^b. 10(11)+5(VI)
Bancroft's School, Woodford Green. M. 10(11)+5(VI)
Chigwell School. B(M)^b. 10(11,13)+5(VI)
Ursuline RC High School, Ilford. G. 20(11)+5(VI)

Brentwood School. B(M)^b. 18(11)+5(VI)
Felsted School, Dunmow. B(M)^b. 8(11,13)+5(VI)
Bishop's Stortford College. B(M)^b. 6(11,13)+4(VI)
Friend's School, Saffron Walden. M^b. 20(11,12,13)+5(VI)

South-West

Glos, Avon and Somerset
Wycliffe College, Stonehouse. B(M)^b. 5(11,13)+5(VI)
Bristol Cathedral School, College Green, Bristol. B(M). 20(11)+5(VI)
Bristol Grammar School, University Rd, Bristol. M. 40(11)+5(VI)
Clifton College, Bristol. M^b. 10(11)
Clifton High School, Bristol. G^b. 8(11,13)+5(VI)
Colston's School, Stapleton, Bristol. B(M)^b. 15(11,13)+5(VI)
Colston's Girls' School, Cheltenham Rd, Bristol. G. 20(11)+5(VI)
Queen Elizabeth's Hospital School, Clifton, Bristol. B^b. 25(11)+5(VI)
Redland High School, Redland Court, Bristol. G. 10(11)+5(VI)
Red Maid's School, Westbury-on-Trym, Bristol. G. 25(11)+5(VI)
Bath High School, Lansdown, Bath. G. 18(11)+5(VI)
King Edward's School, North Rd, Bath. B. 16(11,12,13)+2(VI)
Kingswood School, Bath. M^b. 6(11,12,13)+5(VI)
Monkton Coombe School, Nr Bath. B(M)^b. 5(11,13)+5(VI)
Wells Cathedral School, M^b. 11(11,12,13)+4(VI)
Bruton School for Girls, Somerset. G^b. 20(11)+5(VI)
Taunton School. M^b. 6(11)+5(VI)
Queen's College, Taunton. M^b. 10(11,12,13)+4(VI)
Wellington School, Somerset. M^b. 35(11,13)+5(VI)

Devon and Cornwall
Truro High School, Falmouth Rd, Truro. G^b. 10(11)+5(VI)
Truro School, Trennick Lane, Truro. B(M)^b. 15(11)+5(VI)
Plymouth College, Ford Pk, Plymouth. B(M)^b. 30(11,13)+5(VI)
Exeter School. B^b. 25(11,12,13)+5(VI)
Maynard School, Exeter. G. 26(11,12)+5(VI)
Edgehill College, Bideford, G^b. 20(11)+2(VI)
West Buckland School, Nr Barnstaple. B(M)^b. 12(11,13)+2(VI)

Dorset and Wiltshire
Talbot Heath School, Bournemouth. G^b. 25(11,12,13)+5(VI)
Canford School, Wimborne. B(M). 5(13)+5(VI)
Dauntsey's School, West Lavington, Nr Devizes. M^b. 10(11,13)

APPENDIX I

East Anglia

Wisbech Grammar School. M. 50(11,13)+5(VI)
The Leys School, Cambridge. B(M)^b. 5(11,13)+2(VI)
Perse School for Boys, Cambridge. B^b. 12(11,13)+5(VI)
Perse School for Girls, Cambridge. G. 15(11)+5(VI)
St Mary's RC School, Bateman St, Cambridge. G(M)^b. 15(11)+5(VI)
Culford School, Bury St Edmunds. B^b. 8(11,13)+2(VI)
Ipswich School, Henley Rd, Ipswich. B^b. 10(11)+5(VI)
Ipswich High School, Westerfield Rd, Ipswich. G^b. 24(11)+5(VI)
St Joseph's RC College, Birkfield, Ipswich. B(M)^b. 10(11)+5(VI)
Woodbridge School, Suffolk. M^b. 16(11)+5(VI)
Norwich High School, Newmarket Rd, Norwich. G. 30(11,12)+5(VI)
King Edward VI School, The Close, Norwich B. 18(11,12)+2(VI)
Gresham's School, Holt Norfolk. M^b. +5(VI)

West Midlands

Warwick School. B^b. 25(11,12,13)+5(VI)
King's High School, Warwick. G. 30(11)+5(VI)
Coventry School. M. 35(11)+5(VI)
King Edward's School, Birmingham. B. 42(11,13)+5(VI)
King Edward VI High School, Birmingham. G. 25(11)+5(VI)
Wolverhampton Grammar School. G(M). 45(11,13)+5(VI)
Shrewsbury High School, Town Walls, Shrewsbury. G. 14(11)+5(VI)
Hereford Cathedral School. M^b. 35(11,13)+5(VI)
Malvern College, Worcestershire. B^b. 12(11,13)+3(VI)
Alice Ottley School, Worcester. G^b. 10(11)+3(VI)
King's School, Worcester. B(M)^b. 25(11,13)+5(VI)
Royal Grammar School, Worcester. B^b. 37(11,13)+5(VI)
Denstone College, Uttoxeter, Staffs. M^b. 18(11,12,13)+4(VI)
Newcastle-Under-Lyme School, Staffs, M. 68(11,12,13)+5(VI)

East Midlands

Mount St Mary's RC College, Spinkhill, Derbyshire. M^b. 10(11,13)+5(VI)
Repton School, Derby. B(M)^b. 6(11,13)+5(VI)
Trent College, Long Eaton. B(M)^b. 20(11,12,13)+5(VI)
Nottingham High School. B. 20(11)+5(VI)
Nottingham Girls' High School, Arboretum St, Nottingham.
G. 30(11)+5(VI)
Loughborough Grammar School, B^b. 18(11,13)+5(VI)
Loughborough High School. G^b. 14(11,13)+5(VI)
Ratcliffe RC College, Syston, Nr Leicester. B(M)^b. 12(11,13)+2(VI)
Stamford School. B^b. 20(11,12,13)+5(VI)
Stamford High School, G^b. 15(11)+5(VI)

Wellingborough School. M[b]. 10(11,13)+5(VI)
Northampton High School, Derngate, Northampton. G 35(11,13)+5(VI)
Bedford School, Burnaby Rd, Bedford. B[b]. 20(11,13)+3(VI)
Bedford High School, Bromham Rd, Bedford G[b]. 20(11,13)+3(VI)
Bedford Modern School, Manton Lane, Bedford. B[b]. 20(11,13)+3(VI)
Dame Alice Harpur School, Cardington Rd, Bedford. G 20(11,13)+3(VI)

Yorkshire and Humberside

Harrogate College. G[b]. 5(11)+2(VI)
St Peter's School, York. B(M)[b]. 25(11,13)+5(VI)
Pocklington School, Nr York. B[b]. 20(11,13)+3(VI)
Hymers College, Hull. B(M). 28(11,13)+5(VI)
Batley Grammar School, Carlinghow Hill, Batley. B. 40(11,12,13)+5(VI)
Bradford Grammar School, Keighley Rd, Bradford. B. 30(11,13)
Bradford Girls' Grammar School, Squire Lane, Bradford. G 10(11,12,13)
Woodhouse Grove School, Apperley Bridge, Bradford B(M)[b]. 23(11,13)+5(VI)
Leeds Grammar School, Moorland Rd, Leeds. B. 35(11,12,13)+5(VI)
Leeds Girls' High School, Headingley Lane, Leeds. G. 20(11,12,13)+5(VI)
Queen Elizabeth Grammar School, Wakefield. B[b]. 25(11,12)+5(VI)
Wakefield High School. G. 22(11,13)+5(VI)
Sheffield High School, Rutland Pk, Sheffield. G(M). 16(11)+5(VI)

North-West

CUMBRIA AND LANCASHIRE
St Bees School. M[b]. 12(11,13)+5(VI)
Casterton School, Kirkby Lonsdale. G[b]. 8(11,12,13)+4(VI)
Sedbergh School. B[b]. 5(11)+5(VI)
Stonyhurst RC College, Whalley, Blackburn B[b]. 5(11,13)+2(VI)
Queen Elizabeth's Grammar School, Blackburn. B(M). 40(11,12,13)+5(VI)
Rossall School, Fleetwood. M[b]. 6(13)+4(VI)
Arnold School, Blackpool. M[b]. 10(11)+5(VI)
King Edward VII School, Lytham. B. 34(11,13)+5(VI)
Queen Mary School, Lytham. G. 38(13)+5(VI)
Kirkham Grammar School. M. 10(1)+5(VI)

MERSEYSIDE
St Edward's RC College, Sandfield Park, Liverpool. B. 55(11)+5(VI)
Liverpool College, Mossley Hill, B(M)[b]. 25(11)+5(VI)
Belvedere School, Prince's Park, Liverpool. G. 25(11)+5(VI)
St Mary's RC College, Great Crosby B(M). 40(11,13)+5(VI)
Merchant Taylors' School, Crosby. B. 33(11,13)+5(VI)
Merchant Taylors' Girls School, Crosby. G. 23(11)+5(VI)

APPENDIX I

Birkenhead School. B. 40(11,13)+5(VI)
St Anselm's RC College, Birkenhead. B. 30(11)+5(VI)
Birkenhead High School. G. 40(11)+5(VI)
Upton Hall Convent RC School, Wirral. G. 30(11,12,13)+5(VI)

GREATER MANCHESTER AND CHESHIRE
Bolton School (Boys' Division). B. 38(11)+5(VI)
Bolton School (Girls' Division). G. 38(11)+5(VI)
Bury Grammar School (Boys). B. 30(11)+5(VI)
Bury Grammar School (Girls). G. 35(11)+5(VI)
Hulme Grammar School (Boys), Oldham. B. 30(11)+5(VI)
Hulme Grammar School (Girls), Oldham. G. 30(11)+5(VI)
Manchester Grammar School. B. 40(11)+5(VI)
William Hulme's Grammar School, Manchester. B. 30(11)+5(VI)
St Bede's RC College, Alexandra Pk, Manchester. B(M)^b. 30(11)+5(VI)
Manchester High School, Grangethorpe Rd, Manchester G. 25(11)+5(VI)
Withington Girls' School, Fallowfield, Manchester. G. 15(11)+3(VI)
Stockport Grammar School. M. 40(11)+5(VI)
Cheadle Hulme School, Cheadle. M^b. 20(11)+5(VI)
St Ambrose RC College, Hale Barns, Altrincham. B. 15(11)+5(VI)
Loreto Convent RC Grammar School, Altrincham. G. 13(11, 12,13)+5(VI)
The King's School, Macclesfield. B. 30(11,13)+5(VI)
The King's School, Chester B. 16(11)+5(VI)
The Queen's School, Chester. G. 12(11)+5(VI)

North-East

Royal Grammar School, Newcastle upon Tyne. B. 55(11,13)+5(VI)
Dame Allan's Boys' Schools. Newcastle upon Tyne. B. 27(11,12,13)+5(VI)
Dame Allan's Girls' School, Newcastle upon Tyne. G. 20(11)+5(VI)
Central Newcastle High School, Newcastle upon Tyne. G. 18(11)+5(VI)
La Sagesse Convent RC School, Newcastle upon Tyne. G. 25(11)+5(VI)

(Reproduced from *Assisted Places in Independent Schools: A Brief Guide for Parents* (1987) DES.)

Appendix II
Addresses of Local Education Authorities

Authorities in England

AVON
Director of Education
County of Avon
PO Box 57
Avon House North
St James Barton
Bristol BS99 7EB
Tel: 0272 290777

BARKING AND DAGENHAM
Chief Education Officer
Education Offices
Town Hall
Barking
Essex IG11 7LU
Tel: 01-592 4500

BARNET
Director of Educational Services
and Chief Education Officer
Education Department
Town Hall
Friern Barnet
London N11 3DL
Tel: 01-368 1255

BARNSLEY
Education Officer
Education Offices
Berneslai Close
Barnsley
South Yorkshire S70 2HS
Tel: 0226 287621

BEDFORDSHIRE
Director of Education
Education Department
County Hall
Bedford MK42 9AP
Tel: 0234 63222

BERKSHIRE
Director of Education
Education Department
Shire Hall
Shinfield Park
Reading RG2 9XE
Tel: 0734 875444

BEXLEY
Director of Education
Bexley London Borough
Town Hall
Crayford
Kent DA1 4EN
Tel: 01-303 7777

BIRMINGHAM
Chief Education Officer
Education Department
Margaret Street
Birmingham
Tel: 021-235 2551

APPENDIX II

BOLTON
Director of Education and Arts
PO Box 53 Paderborn House
Civic Centre
Bolton
Lancs BL1 1JW
Tel: 0204 22311

BRADFORD
Director of Educational Services
Provincial House
Tyrrell Street
Bradford
West Yorkshire BD1 1NP
Tel: 0274 75211

BRENT
Director of Education
London Borough of Brent
Education Department
PO Box No 1
Chesterfield House
9 Park Lane
Wembley
Middlesex HA9 7RW
Tel: 01-904 1244

BROMLEY
Director of Education
London Borough of Bromley
Education Department
The Town Hall
Tweedy Road
Bromley
Kent BR1 1SB
Tel: 01-464 3333

BUCKINGHAMSHIRE
Chief Education Officer
County Hall
Aylesbury
Bucks HP20 1UZ
Tel: 0296 395000
Telex: 83101

BURY
Director of Education
Education Department
Athenaeum House
Market Street
Bury
Lancs BL9 0BN
Tel: 061-705 5000
Telex: 669853

CALDERDALE
Chief Education Officer
Education Department
PO Box 33
Northgate House
Northgate
Halifax
West Yorkshire HX1 1UN
Tel: 0422 57257

CAMBRIDGESHIRE
Chief Education Officer
Castle Court
Shire Hall
Castle Hill
Cambridge CB3 0AP
Tel: 0223 317111

CHESHIRE
Director of Education
County Hall
Chester CH1 1SQ
Tel: 0244 602330

CLEVELAND
County Education Officer
Education Offices
Woodlands Road
Middlesbrough
Cleveland TS1 3BN

CORNWALL
Secretary for Education
Education Offices
County Hall
Truro
Cornwall TR1 3BA
Tel: 0872 74282

COVENTRY
Director of Education
New Council Offices
Earl Street
Coventry CV1 5RS
Tel: 0203 25555

CROYDON
Director of Education
Taberner House
Park Lane
Croydon CR9 1TP
Tel: 01-686 4433

CUMBRIA
Director of Education
Education Offices
5 Portland Square
Carlisle CA1 1PU
Tel: 0228 24356

DERBYSHIRE
Director of Education
County Offices
Matlock
Derbyshire DE4 3AG
Tel: 0629 3411

DEVON
Chief Education Officer
County Hall
Exeter EX2 4QG
Tel: 0392 77977

DONCASTER
Director of Educational Services
Princegate
Doncaster
South Yorkshire DN1 3EP
Tel: 0302 734104

DORSET
County Education Officer
Education Department
County Hall
Dorchester
Dorset DT1 1XJ
Tel: 0305 251000

DUDLEY
Chief Education Officer
Westox House
1 Trinity Road
Dudley
West Midlands DY1 1JB
Tel: 0384 55433
Telex: 339831

DURHAM
Chief Education Officer
Education Department
County Hall
Durham DH1 5UJ
Tel: 0385 64411

EALING
Chief Education Officer
Hadley House
79-81 Uxbridge Road
Ealing
London W5 5SU
Tel: 01-579 2424

EAST SUSSEX
County Education Officer
PO Box 4
County Hall
St Anne's Crescent
Lewes
East Sussex BN7 1SG
Tel: 0273 475400

ENFIELD
Director of Education
Education Department
PO Box 56
Civic Centre
Silver Street
Enfield
Middlesex EN1 3XQ
Tel: 01-366 6565

APPENDIX II

ESSEX
County Education Officer
Education Department
PO Box 47
Threadneedle House
Market Road
Chelmsford CM1 1LD
Tel: 0245 267222

GATESHEAD
Director of Education
Education Department
Civic Centre
Regent Street
Gateshead
Tyne and Wear NE8 1HH
Tel: 0632 4771011

GLOUCESTERSHIRE
Chief Education Officer
Shire Hall
Gloucester GL1 2TP
Tel: 0452 425300

HAMPSHIRE
County Education Officer
The Castle
Winchester
Hampshire SO23 8UG
Tel: 0962 54411

HARINGEY
Chief Education Officer
London Borough of Haringey
Education Offices
48 Station Road
London N22 4TY
Tel: 01-881 3000

HARROW
Director of Education
PO Box 22, Civic Centre
Station Road
Harrow
Middlesex HA1 2UW
Tel: 01-863 5611

HAVERING
Director of Educational Services
London Borough of Havering
Education Department
Mercury House
Mercury Gardens
Romford RM1 3DR
Tel: 0708 66999

HEREFORD AND WORCESTER
County Education Officer
Castle Street
Worcester WR1 3AG
Tel: 0905 353366

HERTFORDSHIRE
County Education Officer
County Hall
Hertford SG13 8DG
Tel: 0992 555818

HILLINGDON
Director of Education
London Borough of Hillingdon
Civic Centre
Uxbridge
Middlesex UB8 1UW
Tel: 0895 50111

HOUNSLOW
Director of Education
Civic Centre
Lampton Road
Hounslow
Middlesex TW3 4DN
Tel: 01-570 7728

HUMBERSIDE
Director of Education
Education Department
County Hall
Beverley
North Humberside
HU17 9BA
Tel: 0482 867131

INNER LONDON EDUCATION
AUTHORITY
Education Officer and Chief
Executive
County Hall
London SE1 7PB
Tel: 01-633 5000

ISLE OF WIGHT
County Education Officer
County Hall
Newport
Isle of Wight PO30 1UD
Tel: 0983 524031

ISLES OF SCILLY
Secretary for Eduction
Council of the Isles of Scilly
Town Hall
St Marys
Isles of Scilly TR21 0LW
Tel: 0720 22537

KENT
County Education Officer
Education Department
Springfield
Maidstone
Kent ME14 2LJ
Tel: 0622 67141

KINGSTON UPON THAMES
Director of Education and
Recreation
Royal Borough of Kingston upon
Thames
Guildhall
High Street
Kingston Upon Thames
Surrey KT1 1EU
Tel: 01-546 2121
Fax: 01-549 2889

KIRKLEES
Director of Educational Services
Kirklees Metropolitan Council

Oldgate House
2 Oldgate
Huddersfield
HD1 6QW
Tel: 0484 537399

KNOWSLEY
Borough Education Officer
Knowsley Borough Council
Education Office
Huyton Hey Road
Huyton
Liverpool L36 5YH
Tel: 051-480 5111

LANCASHIRE
Chief Education Officer
PO Box 61
County Hall
Preston PR1 8RJ
Tel: 0772 54868

LEEDS
Director of Education
Education Offices
Leeds Education Department
Selectapost 17
Merrion House
Merrion Centre
Leeds LS2 8DT
Tel: 0532 463000

LEICESTERSHIRE
Director of Education
Education Department
County Hall
Glenfield
Leicester LE3 8RF
Tel: 0533 871388

LINCOLNSHIRE
Director of Education
County Offices
Newland
Lincoln LN1 1YQ
Tel: 0522 552222

LIVERPOOL
Director of Education
Education Offices
14 Sir Thomas Street
Liverpool L1 6BJ
Tel: 051-236 5480

MANCHESTER
Chief Education Officer
Education Offices
Crown Square
Manchester M60 3BB
Tel: 061-234 5000

MERTON
Director of Education and
Recreation
London Borough of Merton
Crown House
London Road
Merton
Surrey SM4 5DX
Tel: 01-543 2222

NEWCASTLE UPON TYNE
Director of Education
Education Offices
Civic Centre
Barras Bridge
Newcastle upon Tyne
NE1 8PU
Tel: 091-2328520

NEWHAM
Director of Education
London Borough of Newham
Education Offices
379-383 High Street
Stratford
London E15 4RD
Tel: 01-534 4545

NORFOLK
County Education Officer
County Hall
Martineau Lane
Norwich NR1 2DL
Tel: 0603 611122

NORTHAMPTONSHIRE
County Education Officer
Education Department
Northampton House
Northampton
NN1 2HX
Tel: 0604 256256

NORTHUMBERLAND
Director of Education
Education Department
County Hall
Morpeth
Northumberland NE61 2EF
Tel: 0670 514343

NORTH TYNESIDE
Director of Education
North Tyneside Metropolitan
Borough Council
Education Offices
The Chase
North Shields
Tyne and Wear NE29 0HW
Tel: 091-2576621

NORTH YORKSHIRE
County Education Officer
County Hall
Northallerton
North Yorkshire DL7 8AE
Tel: 0609 3123

NOTTINGHAMSHIRE
Chief Education Officer
County Hall
West Bridgford
Nottingham NG2 7QP
Tel: 0602 823823

TEACHERS, PARENTS AND GOVERNORS

OLDHAM
Director of Education
Education Department
Old Town Hall
Middleton Road
Chadderton
Oldham OL9 6PP
Tel: 061-678 4200

OXFORDSHIRE
Chief Education Officer
Education Department
Macclesfield House
New Road
Oxford OX1 1NA
Tel: 0865 722422

REDBRIDGE
Director of Educational Services
Education Office
London Borough of Redbridge
Lynton House
255-259 High Road
Ilford
Essex IG1 1NN
Tel: 01-478 3020

RICHMOND UPON THAMES
Director of Education
London Borough of Richmond
upon Thames
Education Department
Regal House
London Road
Twickenham TW1 3QB
Tel: 01-891 1411

ROCHDALE
Chief Education Officer
Education Department
PO Box 70 Municipal Offices
Smith Street
Rochdale OL16 1YD
Tel: 0706 521100

ROTHERHAM
Director of Education
Norfolk House
Walker Place
Rotherham S60 1QT
Tel: 0709 382121

ST HELENS
Director of Community Education
Education Department
Century House
Hardshaw Street
St Helens
Merseyside WA10 1RN
Tel: 0744 24061

SALFORD
Chief Education Officer
Education Office
Chapel Street
Salford M3 5LT
Tel: 061-832 9751
Telex: 669806

SANDWELL
Director of Education
Sandwell Metropolitan Borough
Council
PO Box 41
Shaftesbury House
High Street
West Bromwich
Sandwell
West Midlands B70 0LT
Tel: 021-525 7366

SEFTON
Chief Education Officer
Sefton Borough Council Education
Department
Town Hall
Merseyside L20 7AE
Tel: 051-933 6003

APPENDIX II

SHEFFIELD
Chief Education Officer
PO Box 67
Leopold Street
Sheffield S1 1RJ
Tel: 0742 26341
Telex: 54243

SHROPSHIRE
County Education Officer
The Shirehall
Abbey Foregate
Shrewsbury SY2 6ND
Tel: 0743 254302

SOLIHULL
Director of Education
PO Box 20
Council House
Solihull
West Midlands B91 3QU
Tel: 021-705 6789

SOMERSET
Chief Education Officer
County Hall
Taunton
Somerset TA1 4DY
Tel: 0823 333451

SOUTH TYNESIDE
Director of Education
Education Department
Town Hall
Grange Road
Jarrow
Tyne and Wear NE32 3LE
Tel: 091-4891141

STAFFORDSHIRE
Chief Education Officer
County Buildings
Tipping Street
Stafford ST16 2DH
Tel: 0785 22321

STOCKPORT
Director of Education
Education Division
Stopford House
Town Hall
Stockport
Cheshire SK1 3XE
Tel: 061-480 4949

SUFFOLK
County Education Officer
Education Department
St Andrew House
Grimwade Street
Ipswich IP4 1LJ
Tel: 0473 230000

SUNDERLAND
Director of Education
Education Department
PO Box No 101
Town Hall and Civic Centre
Sunderland SR2 7DN
Tel: 0783 76161
Telex: 537037

SURREY
County Education Officer
County Hall
Penrhyn Road
Kingston upon Thames KT1 2DJ
Tel: 01-541 9501

SUTTON
Director of Education
London Borough of Sutton
The Grove
Carshalton SM5 3AL
Tel: 01-661 5000

119

TAMESIDE
Director of Education
Tameside Metropolitan Borough
Council
Education Department
Council Offices
Wellington Road
Ashton under Lyne
Lancs OL6 6DL
Tel: 061-330 8355
Telex: 669991

TRAFFORD
Chief Education Officer
Trafford Borough Council
PO Box 19
Education Department
Tatton Road
Sale
Trafford M33 1YR
Tel: 061-872 2101

WAKEFIELD
Chief Education Officer
Education Department
8 Bond Street
Wakefield
West Yorkshire WF1 2QL
Tel: 0924 370211

WALSALL
Director of Education
The Civic Centre
Darwall Street
Walsall
West Midlands WS1 1DQ
Tel: 0922 21244

WALTHAM FOREST
Chief Education Officer
London Borough of Waltham
Forest
Leyton Municipal Offices
High Road
Leyton
London E10 5QJ
Tel: 01-527 5544

WARWICKSHIRE
County Education Officer
22 Northgate Street
Warwick CV34 4SR
Tel: 0926 410410

WEST SUSSEX
Director of Education
County Hall
West Street
Chichester
West Sussex PO19 1RF
Tel: 0243 777100

WIGAN
Director of Education
Education Offices
Gateway House
Standishgate
Wigan WN1 1XL
Tel: 0942 827880

WILTSHIRE
Chief Education Officer
County Hall
Bythesea Road
Trowbridge
Wiltshire BA14 8JB
Tel: 0222 143641
Telex: 44340

WIRRAL
Director of Education
Wirral Borough Council
Municipal Offices
Cleveland Street
Birkenhead L41 6NH
Tel: 051-647 7000

WOLVERHAMPTON
Director of Education
Education Department
Civic Centre
St Peter's Square
Wolverhampton WV1 1RR
Tel: 0902 27811

Authorities in Wales

CLWYD
Director of Education
Clwyd County Council
Shire Hall
Mold
Clwyd CH17 6ND
Tel: 0352 2121

DYFED
Director of Education
Dyfed County Council
Education Headquarters
Pibwrlwyd
Carmarthen
Dyfed SA31 3NH
Tel: 0267 233333

GWENT
Director of Education
Education Department
County Hall
Cwmbran
Gwent NP44 2XG
Tel: 06333 838838

GWYNEDD
Director of Education
Gwynedd County Council
Education Offices
Castle Street
Caernarvon
Gwynedd LL55 1SH
Tel: 0286 4121

MID GLAMORGAN
Director of Education
Mid Glamorgan County Council
Education Department
County Hall
Cathays Park
Cardiff CF1 3NF
Tel: 0222 820820

POWYS
Director of Education
Education Department
Powys County Council
The Lindens
Spa Road
Llandrindod Wells LD1 5HA
Tel: 0597 3711

SOUTH GLAMORGAN
Director of Education
South Glamorgan County Council
Education Offices
Kingsway
Cardiff CF1 4J
Tel: 0222 44291

WEST GLAMORGAN
Director of Education
West Glamorgan County Council
Education Department
County Hall
Swansea
West Glamorgan SA1 3SN
Tel: 0792 471111

Authorities outside England and Wales

The reference points for queries outside England and Wales are as follows:

SCOTLAND
The Scottish Education Department
New St Andrew's House
St James Centre
Edinburgh EH1 3SY
Tel: 031-556 8400

NORTHERN IRELAND
Department of Education for
Northern Ireland
Rathgael House
Baloo Road
Bangor
Co Down BT19 2PR
Tel: 0247 466311

CHANNEL ISLANDS
Guernsey
States of Guernsey Educational
Council
PO Box No 32
La Couperderie
St Peter Port
Guernsey
Tel: 0481 710821

Jersey
States of Jersey Education
Committee
PO Box 142
Highlands
St Saviour
Jersey
Tel: 0534 71065 ext 200

ISLE OF MAN
Isle of Man Board of Education
Central Government Offices
Douglas
Isle of Man
Tel: 0624 26262 ext 2125

Armed Forces' Schools

In the case of British Forces' Schools, enquiries should be made to the Service Children's Education Authority (SCEA), at this address:

UK Administrative Organisation
Controller SCEA
Ministry of Defence
Directorate of Army Education
Court Road
Eltham
London SE9 5NR
Tel: 01-859 2112 ext 205

Appendix III
Annual Governors' Report

The arrangements for the yearly report of the school governors are set out in the 1986 Act (Section 30):

30.–(1) The articles of government for every county, voluntary and maintained special school shall provide for it to be the duty of the governing body to prepare, once in every school year, a report ('the governors' report') containing –

(a) a summary of the steps taken by the governing body in the discharge of their functions during the period since their last report; and

(b) such other information as the articles may require.

(2) The articles of government for every such school shall, in particular, require the governors' report –

(a) to be as brief as is reasonably consistent with the requirements as to its contents;

(b) where there is an obligation on the governing body (by virtue of section 31 of this Act)* to hold an annual parents' meeting.

  (i) to give details of the date, time and place for the next such meeting and its agenda;

  (ii) to indicate that the purpose of that meeting will be to discuss both the governors' report and the discharge by the governing body, the headteacher and the local education authority of their functions in relation to the school; and

  (iii) to report on the consideration which has been given to any resolutions passed at the previous such meeting;

*See Appendix IV

(c) to give the name of each governor and indicate whether he is a parent, teacher or foundation governor or was co-opted or otherwise appointed as a governor or is an ex officio governor;

(d) to say, in the case of an appointed governor, by whom he was appointed;

(e) to give, in relation to each governor who is not an ex officio governor, the date on which his term of office comes to an end;

(f) to name and give the address of, the chairman of the governing body and their clerk;

(g) to give such information as is available to the governing body about arrangements for the next election of parent governors;

(h) to contain a financial statement –

  (i) reproducing or summarising the latest financial statement provided for the governing body by the local education authority;

  (ii) indicating, in general terms, how any sum made available to the governing body by the authority in the period covered by the report, was used, and

  (iii) giving details of the application of any gifts made to the school in that period;

(i) to give, in the case of a secondary school, such information in relation to public examinations as is required to be published by virtue of section 8(5) of the 1980 Act;

(j) to describe what steps have been taken by the governing body to develop or strengthen the school's links with the community (including links with the police); and

(k) to draw attention to the information made available by the governing body.

(3) The articles of government for every such school shall –

(a) enable the governing body to produce their report in such language or languages (in addition to English) as they consider appropriate; and

(b) require them to produce it in such language or languages (in addition to English and any other language in which the governing body propose to produce it) as the local education authority may direct.

(4) The articles of government for every such school shall provide for it to be the duty of the governing body of any such school to take such steps as are reasonably practicable to secure that –

(a) the parents of all registered pupils at the school and all persons employed at the school are given (free of charge) a copy of the governors' report;

(b) copies of the report are available for inspection (at all reasonable times and free of charge) at the school; and

(c) where there is an obligation on the governing body (by virtue of section 31 of this Act)* to hold an annual parents' meeting, copies of the report to be considered at that meeting are given to parents not less than two weeks before that meeting.

*See Appendix IV

Appendix IV

Annual Parents' Report

The arrangements for the yearly meeting of the governors with parents of the school are given in Section 31 of the 1986 Act:

31.- (1) Subject to subsections (7) and (8) below, the articles of government for every county, voluntary and maintained special school shall provide for it to be the duty of the governing body to hold a meeting once in every school year ('the annual parents' meeting') which is open to –

(a) all parents of registered pupils at the school;

(b) the headteacher; and

(c) such other persons as the governing body may invite.

(2) The purpose of the meeting shall be to provide an opportunity for discussion of –

(a) the governors' report; and

(b) the discharge by the governing body, the headteacher and the local education authority of their functions in relation to the school.

(3) No person who is not a parent of a registered pupil at the school may vote on any question put to the meeting.

(4) The articles of government for every such school shall provide –

(a) for the proceedings at any annual parents' meeting to be under the control of the governing body;

(b) for any annual parents' meeting at which the required number of parents of registered pupils at the school are present, to be entitled to pass (by a simple majority) resolutions on any matters which may properly be discussed at the meeting;

(c) for it to be the duty of the governing body –

    (i) to consider any resolution which is duly passed at such a meeting and which they consider is a matter for them;

    (ii) to send to the headteacher a copy of any such resolution which they consider is a matter for him; and

    (iii) to send to the local education authority a copy of any such resolution which they consider is a matter for the authority; and

(d) for it to be the duty of the headteacher, and of the local education authority, to consider any such resolution a copy of which has been sent to him, or them, by the governing body and to provide the governing body with a brief comment on it (in writing) for inclusion in their next governors' report.

(5) The articles of government for every county, controlled and maintained special school shall provide for any question whether any person is to be treated as the parent of a registered pupil at the school, for the purposes of any provision of the articles relating to the annual parents' meeting, to be determined by the local education authority.

(6) The articles of government for every aided or special agreement school shall provide for any such question to be determined by the governing body.

(7) The articles of government for every special school established in a hospital shall provide that where the governing body are of the opinion that it would be impracticable to hold an annual parents' meeting in a particular school year they may refrain from holding such a meeting in that year.

(8) The articles of government for every county, voluntary and maintained special school (other than a special school established in a hospital), the proportion of registered pupils at which who are boarders is, or is likely to be, at least 50 per cent, shall provide that where –

(a) the governing body are of the opinion that it would be impracticable to hold an annual parents' meeting in a particular school year; and

(b) at least 50 per cent of the registered pupils at the school are boarders at the time when the governing body form that opinion;

they may refrain from holding such a meeting in that year.

(9) In subsection (4)(b) above 'the required number', in relation to any school, means any number equal to at least 20 per cent of the number of registered pupils at the school.

Appendix V
Annual Parents' Meeting

DES Circular 8/86 included a number of important points relating to the Annual Parents' Meeting. Thus it was pointed out that:

> To ensure that maximum benefit is derived from the meeting, governors will wish to create an atmosphere in which parents can freely express their views, and both governors and parents can participate in full and businesslike discussion. Governors will therefore need to consider carefully which additional persons to invite to the meeting under section 31(1)(c)*. It would obviously be useful for their clerk to attend. There may also be a case for inviting a few non-governor members of the teaching and non-teaching staff, a representative of the LEA (in view of potential comment on the LEA's actions) and, in the case of a secondary school, representatives of the more senior pupils. It is unlikely to be desirable to invite the press or members of the public to attend. The governors' decisions should, in any case, have regard to any views parents may express on the matter.
>
> It is open to parents to raise any matter which concerns them within the scope of section 31(2), which excludes matters with no bearing on the school. The Chairman of the meeting, with authority derived from section 31(4)(a)* has the necessary power to ensure that discussion proceeds in an orderly manner. Particular care will be needed in the handling of anything which involves criticism of a named individual, such as a member of staff. The Chairman should try to ensure that any such discussion is kept calm, positive and reasonably brief. Taking early delivery of the point for further consideration by the governing body or LEA might be the most appropriate solution. The person criticised should be offered the right to reply, either at once if he is present or subsequently to the governing body, the headteacher or the LEA, as appropriate.
>
> Only the power to pass formal resolutions under section 31(4)(b)* is limited by the number in subsection (9). If fewer parents are present, the meeting must still take place. (DES Circular 8/86 Section 13)

---

*See Appendix IV

Appendix VI

Statement of Special Educational Needs

I – Introduction

1. In accordance with section 7 of the Education Act 1981 and the Education (Special Educational Needs) Regulations 1983, the following statement is made by the .... council ("the education authority") in respect of the child whose name and other particulars are mentioned below.

Child

Surname .... Other names ....

Home address ....

....

.... Sex ....

Date of birth .... Religion ....

      Home language ....

Child's parent or guardian

Surname .... Other names ....

Home address .... Relationship to child ....

....

....

---

2. When assessing the child's special educational needs the education authority took into consideration, in accordance with Regulation 8 of the Regulations, the representations, evidence and advice set out in the Appendices to this statement.

APPENDIX VI

II – Special educational needs

(Here, set out in accordance with section 7 of the 1981 Act, the child's special educational needs as assessed by the education authority.)

III – Special educational provision

(Here specify, in accordance with Regulation 10(1)(a), the special educational provision which the education authority consider appropriate to meet the needs specified in Part II.)

TEACHERS, PARENTS AND GOVERNORS

IV — Appropriate school or other arrangements

(Here specify, in accordance with Regulation 10(1)(b), the type of school and any particular school which the education authority consider appropriate for the child or the provision for his education otherwise than at a school which they consider appropriate.)

V — Additional non-educational provision

(Here specify, in accordance with Regulation 10(1)(c), any such additional provision as is there mentioned or record that there is no such additional provision.)

(Signature of authenticating officer)

....

(Date)

A duly authorised officer of the education authority.

....

APPENDIX VI

Appendices to the Statement of Special Education Needs

Appendix A : Parental representations

(Here set out any written representations made by the parent of the child in pursuance of section 5(3)(d) of the Act and a summary which the parent has accepted as accurate of any oral representations so made or record that no such representations were made.)

Appendix B : Parental evidence

(Here set out any written evidence either submitted by the parent of the child in pursuance of section 5(3)(d) of the Act or submitted at his request or record that no such evidence was submitted.)

Appendix C : Educational advice

(Here set out the advice obtained in pursuance of Regulation 4(1)(a).)

Appendix D : Medical advice

(Here set out the advice obtained in pursuance of Regulation 4(1)(b).)

Appendix E : Psychological advice

(Here set out the advice obtained in pursuance of Regulation 4(1)(c).)

Appendix F : Other advice obtained by Education Authority

(Here set out any advice obtained in pursuance of Regulation 4(1)(d) or record that no such advice was sought.)

Appendix G : Information furnished by District Health Authority or Social Services Authority

(Here set out any such information as is mentioned in Regulation 8(d) or record that no such information was furnished.)

Appendix VII

Extract from the 1988 Education Reform Act: The National Curriculum Section

An Act to amend the law relating to education.   [29th July 1988]

BE IT ENACTED by the Queen's most Excellent Majesty, by and with the advice and consent of the Lords Spiritual and Temporal, and Commons, in this present Parliament assembled, and by the authority of the same, as follows:—

PART I

SCHOOLS

CHAPTER I

THE CURRICULUM

Preliminary

1.—(1) It shall be the duty—   *Duties with respect to the curriculum.*
   (a) of the Secretary of State as respects every maintained school;
   (b) of every local education authority as respects every school maintained by them; and
   (c) of every governing body or head teacher of a maintained school as respects that school;

to exercise their functions (including, in particular, the functions conferred on them by this Chapter with respect to religious education, religious worship and the National Curriculum) with a view to securing that the curriculum for the school satisfies the requirements of this section.

(2) The curriculum for a maintained school satisfies the requirements of this section if it is a balanced and broadly based curriculum which—
   (a) promotes the spiritual, moral, cultural, mental and physical development of pupils at the school and of society; and
   (b) prepares such pupils for the opportunities, responsibilities and experiences of adult life.

APPENDIX VII

Part I

Principal provisions

The National Curriculum.

2.—(1) The curriculum for every maintained school shall comprise a basic curriculum which includes—

(a) provision for religious education for all registered pupils at the school; and

(b) a curriculum for all registered pupils at the school of compulsory school age (to be known as "the National Curriculum") which meets the requirements of subsection (2) below.

(2) The curriculum referred to in subsection (1)(b) above shall comprise the core and other foundation subjects and specify in relation to each of them—

(a) the knowledge, skills and understanding which pupils of different abilities and maturities are expected to have by the end of each key stage (in this Chapter referred to as "attainment targets");

(b) the matters, skills and processes which are required to be taught to pupils of different abilities and maturities during each key stage (in this Chapter referred to as "programmes of study"); and

(c) the arrangements for assessing pupils at or near the end of each key stage for the purpose of ascertaining what they have achieved in relation to the attainment targets for that stage (in this Chapter referred to as "assessment arrangements").

(3) Subsection (1)(a) above shall not apply in the case of a maintained special school.

Foundation subjects and key stages.

3.—(1) Subject to subsection (4) below, the core subjects are—

(a) mathematics, English and science; and

(b) in relation to schools in Wales which are Welsh-speaking schools, Welsh.

(2) Subject to subsection (4) below, the other foundation subjects are—

(a) history, geography, technology, music, art and physical education;

(b) in relation to the third and fourth key stages, a modern foreign language specified in an order of the Secretary of State; and

(c) in relation to schools in Wales which are not Welsh-speaking schools, Welsh.

(3) Subject to subsections (4) and (5) below, the key stages in relation to a pupil are as follows—

(a) the period beginning with his becoming of compulsory school age and ending at the same time as the school year in which the majority of pupils in his class attain the age of seven;

(b) the period beginning at the same time as the school year in which the majority of pupils in his class attain the age of eight and ending at the same time as the school year in which the majority of pupils in his class attain the age of eleven;

(c) the period beginning at the same time as the school year in which the majority of pupils in his class attain the age of twelve and ending at the same time as the school year in which the majority of pupils in his class attain the age of fourteen;

(d) the period beginning at the same time as the school year in which the majority of pupils in his class attain the age of fifteen and ending with the majority of pupils in his class ceasing to be of compulsory school age.

(4) The Secretary of State may by order—

(a) amend the foregoing provisions of this section; or

(b) provide that, in relation to any subject specified in the order, subsection (3) above shall have effect as if for the ages of seven and eight there mentioned there were substituted such other ages, less than eleven and twelve respectively, as may be so specified.

(5) The head teacher of a school may elect, in relation to a particular pupil and a particular subject, that subsection (3) above shall have effect as if any reference to the school year in which the majority of pupils in that pupil's class attained a particular age were a reference to the school year in which that pupil attained that age.

(6) In this section—

"class", in relation to a particular pupil and a particular subject, means the teaching group in which he is regularly taught that subject or, where there are two or more such groups, such one of them as may be designated by the head teacher of the school;

"school", except in subsection (5) above and the above definition, includes part of a school.

(7) For the purposes of this section a school in Wales is a Welsh-speaking school if more than one half of the following subjects, namely—

(a) religious education; and

(b) the subjects other than English and Welsh which are foundation subjects in relation to pupils at the school;

are taught (wholly or partly) in Welsh.

4.—(1) It shall be the duty of the Secretary of State so to exercise the powers conferred by subsection (2) below as— *Duty to establish the National Curriculum by order.*

(a) to establish a complete National Curriculum as soon as is reasonably practicable (taking first the core subjects and then the other foundation subjects); and

(b) to revise that Curriculum whenever he considers it necessary or expedient to do so.

(2) The Secretary of State may by order specify in relation to each of the foundation subjects—

(a) such attainment targets;

(b) such programmes of study; and

(c) such assessment arrangements;

as he considers appropriate for that subject.

PART I

(3) An order made under subsection (2) above may not require—

(a) that any particular period or periods of time should be allocated during any key stage to the teaching of any programme of study or any matter, skill or process forming part of it; or

(b) that provision of any particular kind should be made in school timetables for the periods to be allocated to such teaching during any such stage.

(4) An order under subsection (2) above may, instead of containing the provisions to be made, refer to provisions in a document published by Her Majesty's Stationery Office and direct that those provisions shall have effect or, as the case may be, have effect as amended by the order.

(5) An order under subsection (2)(c) above may authorise the making of such provisions giving full effect to or otherwise supplementing the provisions made by the order as appear to the Secretary of State to be expedient; and any provisions made under such an order shall, on being published by Her Majesty's Stationery Office, have effect for the purposes of this Chapter as if made by the order.

Courses leading to external qualifications.

5.—(1) No course of study leading to a qualification authenticated by an outside person shall be provided for pupils of compulsory school age by or on behalf of any maintained school unless the qualification is for the time being approved by the Secretary of State or by a designated body and either—

(a) a syllabus provided by the outside person for the purposes of the course is for the time being approved by such a body; or

(b) criteria so provided for determining a syllabus for those purposes are for the time being so approved.

(2) An approval under this section may be given either generally or in relation to particular cases.

(3) In this section—

"designated" means designated by the Secretary of State;

"outside person", in relation to a school, means a person other than a member of staff of the school.

Appendix VIII

Important Addresses

Advisory Centre for Education
(ACE)
18 Victoria Park Square
London E2 9PB

Assistant Masters and Mistresses
Association (AMMA)
7 Northumberland Street
London WC2N 5DA

Association for Children with
Hearing Difficulties
26 Gilbert Street
London SW1

Business and Technician Education
Council (BTEC)
Central House
Upper Woburn Place
London WC1H 0HH

Careers Research and Advisory
Centre (CRAC)
Hobsons Press (Cambridge)
Bateman Street
Cambridge CB12 1LZ

Centre for Teaching of Reading
University of Reading School of
Education
29 Eastern Avenue
Reading RG1 3RU

Children's Legal Centre
20 Compton Terrace
London N1 2UN

City and Guilds of London Institute
(CGLI)
76 Portland Place
London W1N 4AA

Council for National Academic
Awards (CNAA)
344-354 Gray's Inn Road
London WC1X 8PB

Department of Education and
Science (DES)
Elizabeth House
York Road
London SE1 7PH

Department of Education and
Science PDC
Honeypot Lane
Stanmore
Middlesex HA7 1AZ

Independent Schools Information
Service (ISIS)
56 Buckingham Gate
London SW1E 6AH

MENCAP
123 Golden Lane
London EC1Y 0RT

National Association of Governors
and Managers (NAGM)
81 Rustlings Road
Sheffield S11 7AB

APPENDIX VIII

National Association of Head
Teachers (NAHT)
Holly House
6 Paddockhall Road
Haywards Heath
W Sussex RH16 1RG

National Book League
Book House
45 East Hill
Wandsworth
London SW18 2QZ

National Children's Bureau
8 Wakley Street
London EC1V 7QE

National Confederation of Parent
Teacher Associations (NCPTA)
43 Stonebridge Road
Northfleet
Gravesend
Kent

National Foundation for
Educational Research (NFER)
The Mere
Upton Park
Slough
Berks SL1 2DQ

National Society for the Prevention
of Cruelty to Children (NSPCC)
67 Saffron Hill
London EC1N 8RS

National Union of Teachers (NUT)
Hamilton House
Mabledon Place
London WC1H 9BD

Ombudsman: Commissioner for
Local Administration in England
21 Queen Anne's Gate
London SW1H 9BU

Open University
Walton Hall
Milton Keynes MK7 6AA

Professional Association of
Teachers (PAT)
99 Friargate
Derby DE1 1EZ

Royal Society for the Prevention of
Accidents (ROSPA)
Cannon House
Priory Queensway
Birmingham B4 6BS

School Library Association
Liden Library
Barrington Close
Liden
Swindon SN3 6HF

Secondary Heads Association
Chancery House
107 St Paul's Road
Islington
London N1 2NB

Appendix IX
National Parks

Addresses and telephone numbers of liaison officers

BRECON BEACONS
The Assistant Information Officer
Brecon Beacons National Park
7 Glamorgan Street
Brecon
Powys LD3 7DP
Tel: 0874 4437

DARTMOOR
Youth and Schools Liaison Officer
Dartmoor National Park Authority
Parke
Haytor Road
Bovey Tracey
Newton Abbot
Devon TQ13 9JQ
Tel: 0626 832093

EXMOOR
Assistant Visitor Services Officer
Exmoor National Park Authority
Exmoor House
Dulverton
Somerset TA22 9HL
Tel: 0398 23665

LAKE DISTRICT
Youth and Schools Liaison Officer
National Park Visitor Centre
Brockhole
Windermere
Cumbria
Tel: 09662 3467

NORTHUMBERLAND
Youth and Schools Liaison Officer
Northumberland National Park and Countryside Dept
Eastburn
South Park
Hexham
Northumberland NE46 LBS
Tel: 0434 605555

NORTH YORK MOORS
Youth and Schools Liaison Officer
The Moors Centre
Lodge Lane
Denby
Whitby
North Yorkshire YO21 2NB
Tel: 0287 60540

PEAK DISTRICT
Youth and Schools Liaison Officer
Peak National Park Centre
Losehill Hall
Castleton
Derbyshire S30 2WB
Tel: 0433 20373

PEMBROKESHIRE COAST
Youth and Schools Liaison Officer
Pembrokeshire Coast National Park
County Offices
Haverfordwest
Dyfed SA61 1QZ
Tel: 0437 4591

APPENDIX IX

SNOWDONIA
Youth and Schools Liaison Officer
Snowdonia National Park
Information Service
Penrhyndeudraeth
Gwynedd LL48 6LS
Tel: 0766 770274

YORKSHIRE DALES
Information Officer
Yorkshire Dales National Park
Calvend
Mebden Road
Grassington
Near Skipton
North Yorkshire
Tel: 0756 752748

Glossary

ADVANCED FURTHER EDUCATION (AFE), This phrase refers to courses of higher education in institutions other than universities, eg polytechnics and colleges of higher education.

ADVISER, Normally refers to 'professional' staff employed by LEAs to advise on subject and phase aspects of education, to run courses and assist in the appointment of staff. They are sometimes referred to as LEA Inspectors in contrast to the National Inspectors (HMI) employed by the Department of Education and Science.

AGREED SYLLABUS, Following the 1944 Act, LEAs were obliged to draw up non-denominational schemes for the teaching of religious education in maintained schools. The schemes were arrived at after consultation with religious interests, often with an interchange of ideas with other LEAs.

AIDED SCHOOL, This term refers to voluntary, usually denominational schools (eg Church of England, Roman Catholic, Methodist) where there is an agreed sharing of responsibility between the LEA and the School Governing Body (*see* p 13). The school premises are owned by the voluntary body but the running expenses are met by the LEA. The voluntary body has considerable power over teaching appointments, but must contribute 15 per cent of capital costs of additional building work.

A LEVEL, The General Certificate of Education (GCE) at Ordinary Level has, since 1988, been replaced by the New General Certificate of Secondary Education, for pupils at the 16-plus level. The Advanced Level of the GCE has however been retained, along with the recently introduced Advanced Supplementary Level examination which is approximately equivalent to 'half' an A level (*see* p. 78).

ADVISORY CENTRE FOR EDUCATION (ACE), This is an organisation which is non-profit making, and which, through its journal *Where*, supplies independent information on many school topics.

ASSISTANT EDUCATION OFFICER (AEO), Local education authority professional staffing comprises a Chief Education Officer (CEO), often a deputy CEO, and also a number of Assistant Education Officers. AEOs usually have specific sectional duties, eg responsibility for further education.

ASSISTED PLACES, These are places which, since 1981, independent schools may offer to academically able children whose parents are unable to afford public school fees (*see* p. 64).

ARTICLES OF GOVERNMENT, These are the regulations which detail the duties of school governors (*see* p. 85 and 100).

ASSESSMENT OF PERFORMANCE UNIT (APU), Allied to the Department of Education and Science, this Unit was established in 1974 in order to monitor and assess the performance of schoolchildren in a range of areas of experience.

BACHELOR OF EDUCATION (BEd), This is the professional degree commonly taken by intending teachers after a three- or four-year course at an institution of higher education. Holders of the degree acquire qualified teacher's status from the Department of Education and Science, but this is currently dependent upon the serving of a one-year probationary period in the maintained school sector.

BLOCK GRANT, A grant known as the block grant or rate support grant from the central government to local authorities to assist with the running of local services such as education: the remainder of the total spending budget of local councils is obtained from the local rating system, due to be replaced in 1990 by the new Poll Tax.

BURNHAM COMMITTEE, This committee was established after the First World War under the chairmanship of Lord Burnham, with the object of determining teachers' pay scales. These pay scales became obligatory at national level following the 1944 Education Act and were commonly known as the 'Burnham Scales'. The Burnham negotiating committee was abolished in 1987, when pay settlements were imposed by the Secretary of State after protracted disagreements between the teaching profession and the Department of Education and Science. In 1988 a Green Paper outlined possible future permanent arrangements for determining teachers' pay and conditions of service (*see* p. 17).

BUSINESS AND TECHNICIAN EDUCATION COUNCIL (BTEC), This council promotes vocational education and administers courses and qualification arrangements covering a considerable range of occupations, eg agriculture, business, construction, hotel and catering, and engineering. The awards are at three levels: BTEC First, BTEC National and BTEC Higher (*see* p. 79).

CERTIFICATE OF PRE-VOCATIONAL EDUCATION (CPVE), This is an attainment certificate for youngsters of 16 and over who undertake a one-year full-time course of work preparation combined with study (*see* p. 79).

CERTIFICATE OF SECONDARY EDUCATION (CSE), This school-leaving examination was introduced in 1965 to cater for pupils generally 'below' the ability band covered by the General Certificate of Education Ordinary Level examination. The examination has been discontinued following the introduction of the General Certificate of Secondary Education in 1988 which is intended to cover the whole range of ability levels at 16-plus.

CHIEF EDUCATION OFFICER (CEO), The Chief Education Officer is the principal professional officer employed by a local education authority (LEA). He or she has general responsibility for the educational system within a county or county borough and usually has a staff of a deputy CEO, Assistant Education Officers for specific areas of education (eg further education) and advisers or local authority inspectors. Sometimes the title Director of Education or County Education Officer is used synonymously with Chief Education Officer.

CIRCULAR 10/65, This famous Circular was issued by the Department of Education and Science in July 1965, with the intention of advising local education authorities on possible forms of re-organisation of secondary education on comprehensive lines, which was the declared policy of the Labour Government of that time.

CITY AND GUILDS OF LONDON INSTITUTE (CGLI), Commonly referred to as 'City and Guilds', the term refers to preparation and examination in vocational courses arranged through the Institute since its inception over a hundred years ago (*see* p. 80).

CLOSED CIRCUIT TELEVISION (CCTV), The term CCTV is used to indicate a television programme which is relayed, by one means or another, in a limited situation. It is often used for lecturing purposes but some of its earlier uses have become outdated with the advent of television recording by means of the video tape recorder (VTR) and latterly the video cassette recorder (VCR).

COLLEGE OF HIGHER EDUCATION (CHE), This refers to institutions which complement university and polytechnic provision and contain a large element of teacher education studies. The majority of CHEs are currently maintained by the local education authority. A small number of 'voluntary' colleges are financed directly through the Department of Education and Science. From 1990, the Government, by virtue of the 1988 Education Act, has stipulated that all CHEs together with all polytechnics, should be centrally funded through a new council known as the Polytechnics and Colleges Funding Council (PCFC).

COMPREHENSIVE SCHOOL, A comprehensive school is designed to cater for secondary age children of all abilities, without separation into 'grammar' 'modern' or 'technical' institutions. Its introduction on a national level was fostered by a Government Circular in 1965 (Circular 10/65) and over 90 per cent of all secondary school children now attend comprehensive schools of one type or another (either from 11-16 or 11-18 years) sometimes in combination with sixth-form or tertiary colleges. The Circular also permitted the introduction of what came to be known as 'middle schools', catering for the intermediate range of 8-12 or 9-13 years of age.

COMPUTER-ASSISTED LEARNING (CAL), CAL is the term used to describe a teaching/learning situation or package which includes the contribution which can be made by a computer, or more usually a miniaturised computer known as a 'micro'.

CONTROLLED SCHOOL, Controlled schools are more properly referred to as Voluntary Controlled Schools. These schools were originally Church Foundations but responsibility for the schools has, under controlled status, been completely transferred to the local education authority, with the proviso that the school governing body must be consulted over the appointment of the headteacher, and teachers of religious knowledge.

COUNTY COUNCIL, County Councils were established towards the end of the nineteenth century with the duty of administering local services including education, and they constitute the local education authority (LEA). The LEA must set up an Education Committee which consists of elected and co-opted members (*see* Education Committee and page 12).

COUNTY SCHOOL, This term refers to primary and secondary schools which have been established and maintained by the local education authority, in contrast to voluntary schools and independent or public schools.

CURRICULUM COUNCIL, The establishment of an advisory body to be known as the Curriculum Council is part of the 1988 Education Act plans for the introduction and development of a national curriculum. Its principal duty will be to advise and make recommendations with reference to the future status of the core and foundation subjects which constitute the national curriculum.

DIRECT GRANT, This term was applied to some secondary (usually grammar) schools which were funded directly by the Department of Education and Science. One of the features of the direct grant schools was the requirement to take a number of places from LEA primary schools. These places were paid for by the LEA. The direct grant system was abolished by the Labour Government in 1976, and the former direct grant schools are now either maintained by the local education authority or have become independent schools.

DIRECTOR OF EDUCATION, *See* Chief Education Officer (CEO).

EDUCATION COMMITTEE, Education Committees are committees of the local council, which is obliged, by virtue of its status as the local education authority, to set up a committee to administer education in its area. Education

Committees consist of elected members, co-opted members and representatives of professional interests, ie teachers. The power to run the education service is, within budget limitations, delegated by the Education Authority to the Education Committee which itself sets up further sub-committees to consider aspects of the service as a whole, eg a schools sub-committee, a further education sub-committee.

EDUCATION PRIORITY AREA (EPA), The term EPA was coined by the Plowden Committee in 1967. Areas designated as EPAs received extra financial help including additional teacher salary allowances.

ENGLISH AS A FOREIGN LANGUAGE (EFL), EFL refers to courses and qualifications which enable non-English speaking foreigners to learn English, usually in establishments termed foreign language schools.

ENGLISH AS A SECOND LANGUAGE (ESL), ESL refers to courses and qualifications which enable teachers to teach English to people whose native tongue is not English, but who reside in an English speaking community.

FROEBEL TEACHING, This refers to the 'kindergarten' idea of Friedrich Froebel (1782-1852) who pioneered concepts relating to the education of very young children and the use of specialised 'toys'.

FULL-TIME EQUIVALENT (FTE), This term is used in connection with staffing quotas in further and higher education, where the actual number of part-time students is quantified to give a working figure in terms of full-time places.

FURTHER EDUCATION (FE), This refers loosely to part-time and full-time education which takes place at post-school level in colleges of further education. Much of the work under this title is below degree level. It includes technician, vocational and leisure studies. Degree level studies come under the heading of advanced further education (AFE).

GENERAL CERTIFICATE OF EDUCATION (GCE), This examination replaced the former School Certificate in 1951 and until 1986 constituted, with the Certificate of Secondary Education, the recognised basis for the school-leaving examination process at the age of 16-plus years. The GCE examination was offered at two levels – the Ordinary Level (O level) and the Advanced Level (A level). Since 1988 the Ordinary Level of GCE has been replaced by the General Certificate of Secondary Education. The Advanced Level of the GCE has, however, been retained (*see* A level and p. 78).

GENERAL CERTIFICATE OF SECONDARY EDUCATION (GCSE), The General Certificate of Secondary Education has now replaced the O level of the General Certificate of Education and CSEs, and after a two-year preparation period the first candidates took the new examination in the summer of 1988 (*see* p. 75).

GIFTED CHILDREN, This term is usually applied to children of high academic ability who may need special provision at school. The phrase is also applied to children who possess artistic, musical or other special talents, and who again may require special provision in the educational system (*see also* Assisted Places p. 64).

GOVERNING BODY (GB), All maintained schools are required by law to have a governing body which has wide general responsibilities in connection with the running of individual schools. Important changes in the constitution and power of the governing bodies have been made in the 1986 and 1988 Education Acts (*see* p. 85).

GRANT, This term usually refers to the amount of money allocated by central government to individual counties and county boroughs. Until 1959 a specific grant was made towards the cost of local authority education services, but this was replaced in April 1959 by a 'block grant'. As a result, a precise allocation of central funds to the local education authority could no longer be guaranteed. The block grant is now referred to as the Rate Support Grant or RSG.

HEADMASTERS CONFERENCE (HMC) This term applies to the conference of headmasters of the established public schools. Members of the Headmasters Conference meet yearly and the title 'HMC School' is usually regarded as a sign of worthiness.

H M INSPECTORS OF SCHOOLS (HMI), Employed by the Department of Education and Science, HMI form a national inspectorate of approximately 485 men and women. They have varied duties including the inspection of individual schools, offering advice to the DES and ministers, co-ordinating national surveys, running in-service courses and maintaining general standards in education. HMI's independent advice has been valued since the beginnings of the inspectorate in 1839 (*see* pp. 51–5).

HIGHER EDUCATION (HE), Higher Education refers to the work undertaken by universities, colleges of higher education and polytechnics, which normally leads to a degree or diploma qualification. Much of the work is on a full-time basis but increasingly, part-time possibilities are becoming part of a changing HE scheme – notably in the provision of 'Access' courses and a relaxation of entry qualifications for mature students.

HIGHER NATIONAL CERTIFICATE, This is a vocational award which was roughly equivalent to a pass degree and has now been replaced by Business and Technician Education Council qualifications (BTEC) (*see* p. 79).

INDEPENDENT SCHOOL, Schools thus described are private education institutions which do not receive any financial help from the LEA or the DES. They may be small local day schools, or famous day and boarding schools with a long-established reputation and distinguished by the term 'public schools'.

IN LOCO PARENTIS, This phrase meaning 'in the place of a parent' is commonly applied to the relationship between teacher and pupil. A teacher is expected to look after his or her pupils in the same way as a careful and wise parent would look after his or her own children.

INSPECTOR, This term may refer either to H M Inspectors who work on a national basis and are employed by the DES, or more loosely to local inspectors and advisers employed by local education authorities.

INSTRUMENT OF GOVERNMENT, Following the 1980 Education Act, this term refers to the formal constitution of the governing body of a school (*see* p. 85).

INTELLIGENCE QUOTIENT (IQ), This term normally refers to the relationship between a child's actual age and his mental age, as determined by a set of standard tests. 'Average intelligence' is regarded as 100 and a person's intelligence quotient is derived by dividing his or her mental age by his or her physical age and multiplying the result by 100.

JUNIOR SCHOOL, This normally refers to a maintained school which, within the overall primary age range of 5-11 years, caters for pupils of 7-11 years of age. In this case the junior school is administered separately from the infant school; often, however, the 5-11 age range is catered for in a joint junior mixed and infant school (JMI school).

LUMP SUM, Teachers and college lecturers' pensions consist of an annual pension, paid monthly, and a lump sum, paid on retirement. The pension is calculated as one-eightieth of the best salary of the last three years of service multiplied by the number of years and days of reckonable service. The lump sum is calculated as three-eightieths of the best salary, again multiplied by the number of years of reckonable service. The normal 'maximum' of reckonable service is 40 years up to the age of 60, which would result in a half-salary pension.

MAINTAINED SCHOOL, Schools run by the local education authorities are known as maintained schools, in contrast to private, independent schools. Schools which have been set up by the LEA itself are generally referred to as county schools. Voluntary aided and voluntary controlled schools, which are largely financed by the LEAs, are also referred to as maintained schools, as are schools for special educational needs (*see* pp. 12-13).

MENTAL AGE (MA), An 'average' child has a mental age which corresponds to his or her chronological age. Following a series of standardised tests, a child may be assessed as possessing a mental age which is either higher or lower than the average mental age. The intelligence of a child is often stated as an 'intelligence quotient' (IQ) and is simply the ratio between chronological age and mental age. An average child is regarded as possessing an IQ of 100.

MIDDLE SCHOOLS, Following the wide-scale introduction of comprehensive schooling in the 1960s, a number of LEAs began to replace the traditional 'two-tier' system of primary and secondary education with a three-tier system. Under these arrangements children spend the first two or three years of schooling in a primary school (from 5-7 or 5-8 years) and then proceed to a middle-tier school (from 8-12 or 9-13 years), before completing their education in the secondary or third-tier schools (from 12-16 or 13-16 years). In the late 1970s the total number of middle schools was approximately 1,400, but falling rolls at the present time have led a number of LEAs to revert to a two-tier system.

MINISTER OF EDUCATION, The 1944 Education Act replaced the earlier Board of Education with a full Ministry of Education headed by a Minister of State. In 1964 this Ministry was rechristened the Department of Education and Science (DES) headed by a senior minister known as the Secretary of State and assisted by two or three junior ministers.

MIXED ABILITY, This term refers to a type of school organisation in which children of a wide range of ability are taught together in the same class rather than in separate 'ability groups' or 'streams'.

NURSERY CLASS, This is a pre-five-year-old class which is attached to an infants or an infants/junior primary school. Expansion of nursery class provision at the national level has been hindered by financial restraints, lack of premises and shortages of qualified staff.

NURSERY SCHOOL, Nursery schools cater for the two to five age range of children and differ from nursery classes in that they occupy separate premises. Increases in the number of local authority maintained nursery schools have been proposed on many occasions but financial stringencies have hampered national provision.

NATIONAL CURRICULUM, The Secretary of State for Education and Science under the Conservative Government of 1987, proposed the establishment of a national curriculum of core and foundation subjects to be taught in all schools. The proposals were embodied in an Education Bill which, under the title of the Education Reform Bill, became an Act in July 1988 (*see* p. 24).

OPEN UNIVERSITY (OU), The idea of a 'University of the Air' or 'Open University' was conceived by Harold Wilson in 1966. It received its Charter in 1971 and provides courses based upon a combination of correspondence course methods, specially planned textbooks, seminars and television programmes. Based at Milton Keynes, it has been highly successful in recruiting students for courses at degree level, but the original idea of extending the higher education participation rate to a wider section of the community has only been partly realised to date.

PARENT TEACHER ASSOCIATION (PTA), In recent years the greatly increased interest of parents in schools which their children attend, has led to the establishment of Parent Teacher Associations and also to the founding of a National Confederation of Parent Teacher Associations (*see* p. 139).

PERMANENT SECRETARY TO THE DEPARTMENT OF EDUCATION AND SCIENCE, The Permanent Secretary is the senior civil servant in the DES and is ultimately responsible for the advice given by the DES to the Secretary of State.

PHONICS, This term is usually used in connection with schemes for teaching children to read. A phonic system bases itself upon a word build up from the sounds of individual syllables in a word.

PLOWDEN, The Plowden Report of 1967 entitled *Children and their Primary Schools* was commissioned by the Central Advisory Council and had a seminal influence upon the conceptual and developmental ideas upon which the best primary school practice is based.

POLYTECHNICS AND COLLEGES FUNDING COUNCIL (PCFC), Under the 1988 Education Act, the financing of polytechnics and LEA colleges of higher education is to be transferred to a Central Funding Council in 1990. Local 'control' of these institutions ceases on that date and it is anticipated that a more centralised disposition of courses offered will result.

POLYTECHNIC, Polytechnic colleges are institutions which offer a wide range of post A level courses on a full-time, part-time or sandwich basis to students in technical, vocational and liberal studies. Financed by the LEAs, they have often been considered a rival to the university system and nicknamed the 'comprehensive universities'. From 1990, control of the Polytechnics is to be transferred from the LEAs to a Central Funding Council known as the Polytechnics and Colleges Funding Council (PCFC).

POST GRADUATE CERTIFICATE OF EDUCATION (PGCE), This qualification is awarded to graduates who successfully complete a one-year teacher training course in a college or university.

PROGRAMMED TEACHING/LEARNING, These terms were originally used with reference to 'teaching machines' where items of instruction were arranged in small logically progressive steps to assist learning processes. The original programming machines – 'teaching machines' – have now been superseded by computer and micro-computer programmes with the advent of micro-electronics.

PROJECTS, Where schools engage for part of the timetable upon a comprehensive study of a specific topic, rather than individual subject lessons, this is usually termed a project. Items from individual subjects all make a contribution to the complete project which can arouse the interest and enthusiasm of pupils in a different context from the normal 'lesson', especially as the teacher is seen in the role of a guide rather than a tutor.

PROBATIONARY YEAR, After the successful completion of a teacher training course, teachers in maintained schools undergo a probationary period of one year in their first teaching post. At the end of the first year's teaching their Qualified Teacher status is confirmed by the Department of Education and Science on the advice of the employing LEA. The Government has proposed that, from 1989, the probationary year system should be discontinued.

PROFESSIONAL ASSOCIATION OF TEACHERS (PAT), This association was set up as an alternative to existing teacher unions (NUT, NAS/UWT, NAHT). It strongly stressed the professional aspects of the teachers' role rather than the 'negotiating' aspects which had tended to dominate teacher politics. It is committed to a no-strike policy, in the interests of pupils, and has a current membership of approximately 43,000.

PUBLIC SCHOOL, *See* Independent School; *and* Assisted Places.

RATE SUPPORT GRANT (RSG), *See* Block Grant.

REGIONAL ADVISORY COUNCIL (RAC), Regional Advisory Councils for Further Education are voluntary bodies with a responsibility for providing advice on the regional provision of further education courses.

REGISTRATION (OF INDEPENDENT SCHOOLS), All schools in the United Kingdom are subject to inspection by H M Inspectors, whether they have maintained or independent status. All new independent schools must be 'registered' with the DES. Provisional registration is first given to a new school and the registration becomes final following a satisfactory visit from H M Inspectors.

RELIGIOUS EDUCATION (RE), All maintained schools are required to include religious education in their timetable. Religious education is also regarded as an integral part of the National Curriculum, which comes into effect in 1989. County schools must adhere to a non-denominational approach through an 'agreed syllabus' for the region. Voluntary schools follow their own denominational approach, eg Roman Catholic, Church of England, Methodist.

SCHOOL-LEAVING AGE (SLA), children may legally leave school at the age of 16, but they may only do so on specified dates. Thus pupils must stay at school until the end of the Spring term if their 16th birthday falls on any day from the 1 September to 31 January. If their 16th birthday falls between 1 February and 31 August they can leave any time after the Friday before the last Monday in May (normally the Spring Bank Holiday) (*see* p. 70).

SENTENCE METHOD, The process whereby individual children learn to read is not yet fully understood and most teachers use a combination of techniques:

- the phonic method (see also *phonics*, p. 150)
- the look and say method
- the sentence method – the basis of this approach relies upon the assumption that a sentence or clause forms the basis of comprehension and understanding and therefore should be 'grasped' by the reader as a whole.

SPECIAL AGREEMENT SCHOOLS, Special agreement schools constitute only a small proportion of the total voluntary school provision in England and Wales. As a result of a 'special interest' the LEAs pay between roughly a half and three-quarters of the cost of building the new voluntary school or extending an existing one. The voluntary body has the right of appointing the majority of governors and also controls religious instruction in the school. The LEA has the power to appoint teachers but usually there is substantial delegation to the governing body.

SPECIAL EDUCATIONAL NEED (SEN), The original 1944 Act definition of special need categories (SET) has, following the Warnock Report of 1978, been replaced by the wider concept of special needs – a term which may at any given time apply to as many as a fifth of the school population (*see* p. 66).

SPECIAL EDUCATIONAL TREATMENT (SET), *See* Special Educational Need.

STATEMENTING, This refers to the process whereby an LEA identifies and assesses children with special educational needs. The LEA, under the 1981 Education Act, is responsible for preparing, after consultation, a statement which then forms the basis of its proposed actions to cater for the child (*see* p. 66 and Appendix VI).

STREAMING, This refers to a school organisation, usually at secondary level, in which children are grouped into classes according to their abilities, in contrast to an organisation which adopts a mixed ability class grouping.

TECHNICAL AND VOCATIONAL INITIATIVE (TVEI), In conjunction with the Manpower Services Commission (MSC) – renamed the Training Commission – the DES has worked on a number of projects which have been financed by MSC and are designed to explore the methods of planning work at school for pupils in the 14-18 age range, related to the needs of adult and working life.

VICE CHANCELLOR (VC), The Executive Head or Principal of a university, as opposed to the Chancellor who is the 'ceremonial' figurehead.

VOLUNTARY AIDED SCHOOL, The school premises of a Voluntary Aided school are owned by a voluntary group, usually a religious denominational body such as the Roman Catholic Church, the Church of England or the Methodist Church. The running costs of the school are met by the LEA, but the voluntary body has a considerable say in the appointment of staff and in the pupil admission arrangements. Eight-five per cent of 'capital' costs are paid by the DES in connection with alteration and/or extension costs etc (*see* p. 13).

VOLUNTARY CONTROLLED SCHOOLS, These schools have a similar standing to voluntary aided schools (*see* p. 13), but the voluntary body has surrendered all responsibility for maintaining the school and the LEA has an increased say in the appointment of teachers, apart from teachers of religious instruction.

YOUTH TRAINING SCHEME (YTS), The Youth Training Scheme is open to both unemployed and employed youngsters. All 16-year-old leavers can join YTS schemes. Some 17- and 18-year-olds may join and disabled youngsters are eligible to join the scheme up to the age of 21. The Youth Training Scheme is a voluntary scheme which is based upon planned work experience and training together with a minimum period of 13 weeks further education. Responsibility for the scheme lies with the Training Commission (formerly the Manpower Services Commission (MSC)).

WARNOCK REPORT, This report was the result of the committee of enquiry into the education of handicapped children and young people, and was published in May 1978. Many of its recommendations influenced the 1981 Education Act (*see* p. 66).

Further Reading

DES documents

Assisted Places in Independent Schools: A Brief Guide (1987) DES
Better Schools (1985) DES
Children at School and Problems Related to AIDS (1986) DES
Children with Special Needs Circular 1/83 (1983) DES
Drug Misuse and the Young (1985) DES
Education (No 2) Act 1986 Circular 8/86, DES
Grant Maintained Schools: Draft Guidance (1988) DES
Health Education in Schools (1986) DES
Her Majesty's Inspectors of Schools: Their Purpose and Role (1988) DES
HM Inspectors Today: Standards in Education (1983) DES
Local Management of Schools (Coopers and Lybrand Report) (1988) HMSO
A New Choice of School: City Technology Colleges (1986) DES
The New Examination: A GCSE Guide for Employers (1987) HMSO
Records of Achievement: An Interim Report (1987) HMSO
Safety in Education (1981) Bulletin Series, DES
School Governors: A New Role (1988) DES
School Governors: How to Become a Grant Maintained School (1988) DES
Schoolteachers' Pay and Conditions Document (1987) DES
Schoolteachers' Pay and Conditions of Employment Circular 8/87, DES
Schoolteachers' Pay, Conditions and Pensions (1987) TASC/DES
Sex Education at School Circular 11/87, DES
Shouldn't You Become a School Governor? (1988) DES
Working Together for the Protection of Children from Abuse Circular 4/88, DES

General references

Burgess, T and Sofer, A (1986) *The School Governors' Handbook and Training Guide* Kogan Page
Fowler, W S (1988) *Towards the National Curriculum* Kogan Page
Harding, P (1987) *A Guide to Governing Schools* Harper and Row

The Law of Education (1987) (9th edition) Butterworth and Co
Lee, C M (1986) *Child Abuse* Open University Press
Mann, J F (1979) *Education* Pitman
Partington, J (1984) *Law and the New Teacher* Holt
Pile, W (1979) *The Department of Education and Science* Allen and Unwin
Taylor, Felicity (1986) *Parents' Rights in Education* Longman
Taylor, Felicity (1987) *After School* Kogan Page